GCSE
FINDING OUT ABOUT SOCIETY

Lynn Williams

Head of Humanities
Bosworth Community College, Leics

Unwin Hyman

To Martin

Published by
Unwin Hyman Limited
15–17 Broadwick Street
London W1V 1FP

© Lynn Williams 1987
Reprinted 1988

Designed by Snap Graphics
Cover by Chris McLeod

British Library Cataloguing in Publication Data
Williams, Lynn
    Finding out about society.
    1.   Social sciences—Research
    I.   Title
    300'.72   H62
    ISBN 0-7135-2729-3

Typeset in Great Britain by Tradespools Limited, Frome,
Somerset
Printed and bound in Great Britain

Contents

How to Use this Book

If you are following a social science, sociology or integrated humanities GCSE course you will need to carry out at least one enquiry or piece of individual research. This book aims to introduce you to the main types of research and, through guided examples and activities, to help you to learn the skills needed to do a really good enquiry. The book has been written for students to use themselves without a lot of help from the teacher, but most of the activities are best if done in pairs or if discussed with other students afterwards. As well as giving you practice in the different skills you need, each chapter aims to set out the necessary stages for planning and carrying out your own research. In each chapter these stages are summarised in a checklist at the end. Advice is also given in each chapter on how to write up your results and how to draw conclusions.

What sort of enquiry you are doing, and therefore how you use this book, will depend partly on which exam you are sitting. Some syllabuses say that they want you to do a certain type of research such as a questionnaire survey or an observation; others simply say that they want you to do original research. Your teacher will tell you what you have to do. Most good research will use more than one method. Even if you have to do a questionnaire you will still need to do some background research, perhaps using statistics or other sources that relate to your topic.

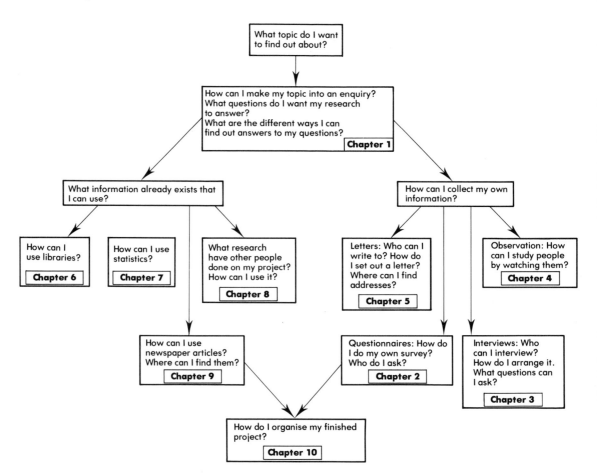

It is important that you *use* this book by picking out the parts which are relevant to you; you do not need to use all of it. Chapter 1, which tells you how to plan your research and helps you decide how to go about it, and Chapter 10, which tells you how to present your finished project are essential, but which other chapters you use apart from these will depend on the types of research you intend to do. The diagram on the left should help you to decide which chapters to use. The chapters, after Chapter 1, can be used in any order. Sometimes words or ideas are introduced which you may not understand. These words are clearly explained the first time that they are used, and are also listed at the back of the book, with the page number where they first appear, so that you can look up the meaning.

At the end of the book is a chapter which talks about how sociologists have used different methods in their own research and the strengths and weaknesses of the different methods for finding out about society. If you are following a sociology course this chapter is important, otherwise you may feel that you do not need to read it.

Doing good research takes a lot of planning and, sometimes, a lot of time. If you take the trouble it is possible for you to find out facts for yourself which you could not get from books or magazines.

A Note to the Teacher

All GCSE Sociology, Social Science and Integrated Humanities courses expect students to carry out an extended piece of individual research as well as completing a number of assignments. The exact requirements of the different syllabuses vary; some give students free choice on the research methods they use whilst others specify exactly what sort of research is to be done.

All of the syllabuses stress the importance of the research process. The completed project is not expected to be long, but is expected to demonstrate an ability to use different methods of research.

This book is written for students. It is to help them practise the skills needed to do a good piece of research and to show them some of the problems to be avoided. It is intended that students should *use* the book by themselves (or in small groups) so that they can concentrate on the skills which they need for their own research. Many of the activities are in fact best done in pairs or small groups so that students can discuss their answers and so learn from each other. It is quite possible to use each chapter with a larger group or whole class in a more formal way if this is desired.

It is intended that the book should be used by students of all ability levels. It provides both basic guidance in research methods and advice on how to use more difficult sources. These are as diverse as *New Society* and census statistics and are for those who wish to develop their research.

Although the book aims primarily to teach the skills required for the research topic it is possible to adapt some sections — especially parts of Chapters 6–9 — to provide self contained assignments which meet the coursework demands of the syllabuses.

Students following a sociology course will not only need to practise the different research skills but will also need to be able to discuss the way in which methods have been used by different sociologists. The Appendix has been written with these students in mind.

I have always found that students are eager to carry out their own research and are keen to use a range of different methods. However, without clear guidance on how to use different methods the final piece of research can be disappointing. To teach all research skills to all students would be extremely time consuming, yet to teach only a few methods would restrict student choice unnecessarily. The aim of this book is, therefore, to enable students individually to practise the skills which they need for their own personal projects.

Chapter One
Choosing a Topic to Study

1 ASKING QUESTIONS ABOUT SOCIETY

If you have done a project before you have probably started with a topic, such as pollution or drugs, and have set out to find information on it. A social science or sociology enquiry must begin, not with a topic, but with a set of questions about that topic which you want to answer. The questions must have something to do with people and their behaviour in society, and answering them must involve you in doing some research of your own. It is important that these are questions that you don't already know the answers to, or that you can't answer simply by referring to books.

One way of finding the questions to ask is to write down every question that you can think of on a topic. This is known as a **THOUGHT EXPLOSION DIAGRAM**.

EXAMPLE: SEX EQUALITY IN EDUCATION

Notice that all of these are quite broad questions; you can't answer them in one or two sentences. Notice also that many of these can only be answered by going out and asking people questions or by observing how people behave.

EXAMPLE: DRUG ABUSE

ACTIVITY

Try to draw up a thought explosion diagram for two of the following topics:

- Television and young children
- Football hooliganism
- The police
- Unemployment
- Racial prejudice
- Political attitudes
- Teenagers or youth culture
- Crime
- Sex equality in the home or at work

Whichever topics you choose, do not try to cover everything; pick out the most important questions.

2 PROBLEMS IN CHOOSING A TOPIC TO STUDY

When doing your own research there are two problems you must avoid:

- You must make sure that your topic is a genuine social science topic, and not just a factual or technical topic such as cars or motorbikes. A social science topic is one which asks questions about people in society. For example, how people's experiences differ depending on their age, sex, race or social class, or how people are influenced by parts of society such as the family, schools or the mass media.
- You must also make sure that the questions which you ask are not straightforward ones which can be answered simply by drawing up lists or copying out facts.

We can understand these two problems better by looking at ways in which sport could be studied as a topic. It is wrong to do a project on sport and just write down the rules, league tables, World Cup winners etc. However, sport as a topic could be acceptable if you see it as part of what people do in their leisure time. You could perhaps look at class or sex differences, or at an issue such as sport advertising or sport on television. The following two examples should make these points clearer.

EXAMPLE: SPORT ON TELEVISION

This could be the beginning of a good enquiry because:

- The questions are fairly open ended and you would have to do a lot of your own research to get answers to these questions.
- It fits in quite well with social science issues like leisure and entertainment and allows us to see if there are any differences between different groups of people.

EXAMPLE: FOOTBALL

This could never be made into a good project because:

- All of the questions are closed; there is only one right answer. It is acceptable to have some closed questions, but most must be open.
- The only research necessary is to read books or football magazines; these might be very useful methods of research in an enquiry but there must also be some personal enquiry such as questionnaires or observation.
- Although it might tell you something about the sport itself, it says nothing about people in society; it is not a social science topic.

Which of the following topics are acceptable as social science enquiry topics? Which are unacceptable? Why?

- Poverty
- Divorce
- Fishing
- Computer games
- Nuclear weapons
- China
- Religion

- Attitudes towards marriage
- Motor racing
- Computer technology
- Socialism
- Experiences at work
- The weather
- Attitudes towards childrearing

Now choose two topics of your own and draw up a thought explosion diagram for each of them. Look at your diagrams before reading on. Check, are your questions purely factual? Can your questions be answered without you doing any research? Do you already know the answers?

If your answer is 'yes' to any of these, scrap them and start again. (It is useful at this stage to get at least one other person to look at your thought explosion diagrams. They may have suggestions for improvement.)

3 PICKING OUT YOUR MAIN ENQUIRY QUESTIONS

When you have got a list of questions on a topic you must put them in order. Which ones are most important? Are they all relevant? You may have far too many questions to answer in one project. For example, it is too much to look at the position of women in the home, in work, in education and in the media; you must pick the area on which you want to concentrate.

You should have drawn up four thought explosion diagrams. For two of these pick out the main and secondary questions as in the examples below.

EXAMPLE: SEX EQUALITY IN EDUCATION
Main question: Do boys and girls have the same opportunities in education?
Secondary questions: What differences are there in exam success and in subject choice between boys and girls? Why do these differences exist? Do teachers treat boys and girls differently?

EXAMPLE: DRUG ABUSE
Main question: How big is the problem of drug abuse in Britain today?
Secondary questions: What is drug abuse — should we include alcohol and tobacco? What sort of people abuse drugs? Is the media presentation of drug abuse correct?

EXAMPLE: SPORT ON TELEVISION
Main question: Is there too much sport on television?
Secondary questions: How does sport on television affect what people do in their leisure time? Does watching sport on television increase or decrease the chance that people will watch the game live? Can sport on television persuade more people to take part in the sports themselves? Are there differences in opinions on sport on television between different groups such as determined by age, sex, and social class?

4 WRITING A HYPOTHESIS

Having got to this stage you need to write your questions as a **HYPOTHESIS**. This is just a statement of what you expect to find out. Your hypothesis might be completely wrong, but this is something that you will discover when you do your research. (In fact, some of my hypotheses below would be proved wrong by research.)

EXAMPLE: SEX EQUALITY IN EDUCATION
Hypothesis: Boys and girls do not have the same opportunities in education. Teachers, parents and pupils themselves have different expectations of male and female students and this influences boys and girls in their subject choices and in their attitude towards school.

EXAMPLE: DRUG ABUSE
Hypothesis: Drug abuse in Britain is on the increase. The typical drug addict is a male middle class teenager. Tobacco and alcohol are widely used by people who disapprove of some other drugs.

EXAMPLE: SPORT ON TELEVISION
Hypothesis: Sport on television has very little effect on leisure as a whole. Most people feel that there is too much sport on television; this is especially true of women and people who are not themselves actively involved in sport.

ACTIVITY >

Now write out your hypotheses for the two topics that you have written main questions for. Ask a friend or teacher to check your hypotheses for you and to suggest how you could improve them.

ACTIVITY >

You must now decide what you are going to do your own enquiry about and follow through all of the stages in this chapter until you have a hypothesis which you want to test. Keep all of your rough plans since this will show how your project has developed. You should also keep a diary or log book to show exactly what you are doing at each stage of your project.

FRIDAY 4th NOVEMBER
Wrote to exam boards for information on subjects chosen by boys and girls.
Sat and observed in classroom to get ideas on what to look for in classroom observation. Listed points.
Arranged to observe in two classes next week. Science with 4th year and English with 3rd year.

FRIDAY 11th NOVEMBER
Observed in classrooms. People wanted to know what I was there for — will this affect what they do?
Had to change my list of points to observe.

5 DECIDING WHAT SORT OF RESEARCH TO DO

As well as reading books and writing off for information you will have to do some of your own research. There are many different types of research which you can do. You may use information which already exists such as statistics collected by the government or organisations like schools. Crime statistics, for example, show the age and sex of the typical criminal as well as the types of crimes committed. This type of research is known as analysis of SECONDARY DATA. Alternatively you may wish to get your information from people first hand by using questionnaires, interviews or observation. This type of research is known as the collection of PRIMARY DATA. The different methods which you could use are summarised below.

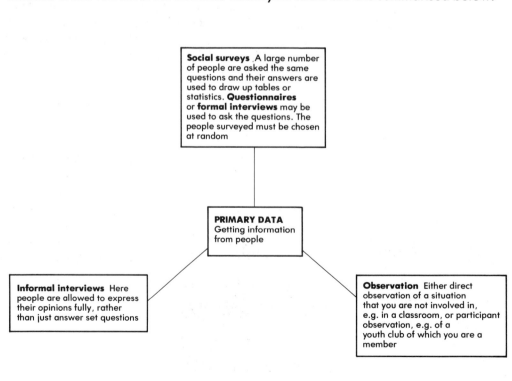

Social surveys A large number of people are asked the same questions and their answers are used to draw up tables or statistics. **Questionnaires** or **formal interviews** may be used to ask the questions. The people surveyed must be chosen at random

PRIMARY DATA
Getting information from people

Informal interviews Here people are allowed to express their opinions fully, rather than just answer set questions

Observation Either direct observation of a situation that you are not involved in, e.g. in a classroom, or participant observation, e.g. of a youth club of which you are a member

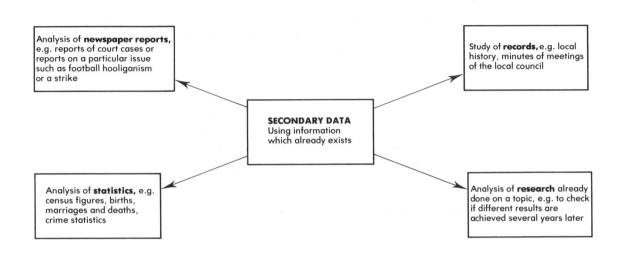

Analysis of **newspaper reports,** e.g. reports of court cases or reports on a particular issue such as football hooliganism or a strike

Study of **records,** e.g. local history, minutes of meetings of the local council

SECONDARY DATA
Using information which already exists

Analysis of **statistics,** e.g. census figures, births, marriages and deaths, crime statistics

Analysis of **research** already done on a topic, e.g. to check if different results are achieved several years later

Which methods you use will depend upon the topic you are studying and what sort of information you want to find out. If your topic is factual and can be measured by figures, e.g. family size or exam subject choice, a questionnaire or published statistics are the best methods. If, however, your topic is more personal, e.g. family relationships or reasons for subject choice, informal interviews or observation might be more useful. If you want to find out facts and figures you are likely to analyse statistics and/or carry out a survey, but if you want to collect more detailed information on what people believe and why they act in a certain way you will use informal interviews or observation. Observation may also be used to find out how people really act rather than how they think they do.

It is quite likely that you will use two or more methods of research in one project. The table below shows some of the possible types of research that could be used to test each of the three hypotheses mentioned earlier.

TOPIC	TYPES OF RESEARCH

Sex equality in education

- Analysis of statistics from examining boards showing the number of entries for different subjects
- Analysis of option choices made in your own school
- Observation in classrooms
- Questionnaire survey or interviews with students and teachers

TOPIC
Drug abuse

TYPES OF RESEARCH
- Analysis of government figures on the number of addicts
- Questionnaire survey on use of drugs and attitudes
- Analysis of newspaper cuttings
- Write to the Home Office for information
- Interview the drug squad, local police or social workers

SHOCK ISSUE

THE Government has pledged to crack down on heroin in the streets. Yet the Mirror witnessed heroin dealers openly and contemptuously selling their deadly wares to children, in one street just two miles from Westminster.

Children even offered to 'score' on our behalf. One 14-year-old said: "I've done it plenty of times. They'll sell to anyone, you only have to ask for £5, £10, or £15 'draws'.

"But watch out, it can get hot here. Park your car away from the road. The police sometimes drive around and take numbers. But if you're careful, there's no problem." The Mirror did not have to ask for drugs. As we entered the road we were repeatedly offered 'smack'.

At one house a red-haired woman left the premises by the back gate pushing her child in a pram.

As she went out through the hole in the fence a continuous file of people went in to "score" at the houses.

We followed two 15 year olds as they left the place through the back fence and bolted down a side alley into a waiting mini driven by another youth. They drove three miles

LOOKOUT: An addict at the house used by heroin pushers.

Sport on television

GRANDSTAND 12.15 5.5 pm

Introduced by Desmond Lynam ● Featuring World Ski-ing Championships

- Analysis of newspaper coverage
- Analysis of television ratings figures
- Questionnaire survey
- Interview people with a specialist interest e.g. football managers
- Content analysis of television coverage

Ski-ing: downhill-racer Pirmin Zurbriggen defends his world title at Crans-Montana

Timetable*
12.20 Ski-ing
12.55 Racing
1.10 Football Focus
1.25 Racing
1.40 Football Focus
2.5 Racing
2.20 Snooker
3.50 Half times
3.55 Rugby League
4.35 Final Score
*Timings are subject to alteration

World Ski-ing Championships
The Men's Downhill
Form would suggest the Swiss are best placed to produce the champion. PIRMIN ZURBRIGGEN is of that ilk. DAVID VINE reports from Crans-Montana.

Racing from Cheltenham
1.0 Food Brokers Cutty Sark Four Years Old Hurdle Race (2m)
1.35 Sparplas Windows Novices' H'cap 'Chase (2¼m)
2.10 Holsten Pils 'Chase (3m 1f)
Bolands Cross may be

looking ahead to the Cheltenham Gold Cup.
Commentators
JOHN HANMER
RICHARD PITMAN

Football
Previews of the FA Cup fourth round and Scottish Cup third-round matches and the usual full results service.

International Snooker
The Benson and Hedges Masters
First semi-final, STEVE DAVIS 6-4 to win ante-post.
Commentators TED LOWE
JACK KARNEHM
CLIVE EVERTON

Rugby League
Silk Cut Challenge Cup
Highlights of one of the first-round matches.
Commentators
RAY FRENCH, ALEX MURPHY
Television presentation:
Ski-ing SSR, Switzerland
Racing BOB DUNCAN
Snooker KEITH MACKENZIE
Rugby League KEITH PHILLIPS
Assistant editor BRIAN BARWICK
Producer MARTIN HOPKINS
Editor JOHN PHILIPS

ACTIVITY

For your own topic list all of the possible types of research which you could do. Then choose those which will be most useful.

One approach to your project is to do a **CASE STUDY**. You may decide that, instead of trying to find out general facts based on a large number of people, you want to look at one case, or a small number of cases, in detail. If you choose to do a case study you can use any of the methods discussed in this book, although participant observation and informal interviews are most common. One case study could use several different methods. For example you could use questionnaires, observation and interviews to look at work experiences in a factory or office. You could use newspapers to look in detail at one case of child abuse, or interviews to look at a small number of cases of long term unemployment.

In all of these cases you hope to learn something about the topic in general by looking at one example in detail.

CHECKLIST

- Choose a topic which interests you. This must be something which involves people.

- Draw a thought explosion diagram. This must ask open questions on your topic which you cannot answer without doing your own research.

- From your thought explosion diagram pick out your main and secondary questions; these should be linked in some way. Don't try to research into all of the questions that you first thought of.

- Write out your hypothesis; what do you expect the answers to your questions to be?

- Decide what methods of research will be most useful for your enquiry.

- Keep a diary or log book to show what you are doing at each stage of your project.

- Don't try to do too much; make sure that your questions are not too difficult and do not try to use every single method of research.

- When you have chosen your methods of enquiry, go on to the chapters which tell you how to do that type of research.

Chapter Two
Designing a Questionnaire

A **QUESTIONNAIRE** is a list of questions. It may be sent through the post, given to people to fill in themselves — in a school or shopping area for example — or used as an interview when you ask the questions and record the answers yourself. It is usually used when you want information from a fairly large number of people, so that you can make **GENERAL STATEMENTS** or **GENERALISATIONS**. Examples of generalisations are: 'teenagers prefer Brookside and Eastenders, whereas older people prefer Crossroads and Coronation Street' or 'the responsibility for childcare and housework remains that of the woman even when both husband and wife go out to work'. If you only ask ten people this will tell you very little, but if you ask fifty you may begin to see a general pattern.

Doing a good questionnaire requires a lot of thought and planning. There are four main stages which you must go through:

- What questions are you going to ask?
- Who are you going to ask?
- How are you going to record your answers?
- What are you going to do with your results?

1 ASKING QUESTIONS

1.1 Background research

> CHAPTER 1 <

> CHAPTER 8 <

Before you can write a list of questions you need to carry out some background research into your topic. This will help you to know what questions to ask. You should already have written a hypothesis. You should now read books and leaflets (you may need to write off for these) to gain some knowledge and general ideas on your project. At this stage you could also look at research which other people have done into your topic, or you could look at government statistics which are relevant to your project.

> CHAPTERS 6 & 7 <

1.2 Different types of questions

There are many different kinds of questions and you will probably use several of these in your questionnaire.

Classification questions such as age, sex, occupation. These questions help you to group people when looking at your results. But only ask them if they are relevant to your hypothesis. If you think that people of different ages will give different answers, ask their age; if you think that age makes no difference do not ask this question. Generally it is best to ask age by getting people to tick boxes as shown:
What is your age?

Under 15 ☐ 16–30 ☐ 31–50 ☐ 51 + ☐

Factual questions are straightforward such as: 'how often do you watch Top of the Pops? or 'how much money do you spend on clothes?'.

Knowledge questions are used when you want to find out how much people know on a topic. For example: 'do you know what the law says about abortion?' or 'approximately how many animals are used for experiments every year?'.

Opinion questions are for when you want to find out what someone thinks about an issue such as 'do you think that Britain should give more aid to third world countries?' or 'do you think that the school leaving age should be raised to eighteen?'.

Motivation questions are used when you want to find out why a person does or does not do something. Simple examples are 'why don't you go to football matches?' or 'which political party did you vote for in the last election and why?'.

1.3 Open and closed questions

Many of the questions just given as examples are in fact bad questions because they would be very difficult to analyse. If you want to draw up tables and graphs from your results you need to ask questions where there are only a few answers which people can give; you can then add up the number of people who give each answer and can look for patterns. **CODED-CHOICE QUESTIONS** make this possible. In these questions you make a list of all possible answers and ask people to tick a box rather than writing out an answer. These types of question are also known as closed or **CLOSED-CODED QUESTIONS**. Here are some examples:

How often do you watch Top of the Pops?

Never	☐
Every week	☐
Two or three times a month	☐
Once a month or less	☐

How much money do you spend on clothes each month?

Less than £10	☐
£10–£20	☐
£21 or more	☐

Note that I do not say '£20 or more' since the person who spends £20 will not know which box to tick.

Why don't you go to football matches? (Rank 1–4 in order of importance)

Don't like the game	☐
Prefer to watch it on television	☐
It costs too much money	☐
Worried about the violence	☐
Other reasons (please state)	

Approximately how many animals are used for experiments each year?

11 million   1 million   4 million   500 thousand   Don't know

(Please circle the right answer)

In 1985 the British Government gave approximately £1¼ million in overseas aid. This was 0.34% of the country's total income (GNP). Do you think that this is:

Too much ☐
Too little ☐
About the right amount ☐

If you want people to express their opinions in more detail you should use OPEN QUESTIONS, allowing space for people to write in their answers.

Which party did you vote for in the last election? Why?

— — — — — — — — — — — — — — — — —

— — — — — — — — — — — — — — — — —

1.4 Writing questions: Problems to avoid

There are many problems with questions. Sometimes questions are unclear or use words which the person answering does not understand. Sometimes alternative answers do not allow the person answering to say what they really think. There are five main problems which cause people to write bad questions.

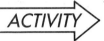

ACTIVITY

Read the following examples carefully and try to rewrite each question to overcome the problems. Sometimes you may need to write two questions rather than one.

LEADING QUESTIONS
- Do you not think that women should not start work until their children are old enough to go to school?
- Don't you agree that there is too much violence on television?

Both of these questions encourage the person answering to say 'yes' because of the way in which they are worded.

PRESUMING QUESTIONS
- When did you last go on holiday?
- How many boyfriends/girlfriends have you had?

Both of these questions assume that this is something that the person answering has done. It would be difficult to answer 'never' or 'none' and the person might be pushed into telling a lie to cover up embarrassment.

DOUBLE QUESTIONS
- Do you think that Britain should spend less money on nuclear weapons and more money on foreign aid?
- Do you think that there is too much sex and violence on television and this is responsible for the lowering of standards in society?

Both of these questions have more than one part — the first is a double question and the second a triple question — but you can only give one answer. You may think that we should spend less on nuclear weapons but not more on foreign aid; there is no way in which you can say this.

QUESTIONS WHERE ANSWER CHOICES ARE UNCLEAR OR VAGUE

● How often do you go to church?

Regularly ☐
Occasionally ☐
Never ☐

Answers to this question are meaningless and could not be compared since we may all mean different things by 'regularly' and 'occasionally'.

● How much money does your family spend on leisure activities each week?

less than £5 ☐
£5–£10 ☐
£10–£15 ☐
£15 or more ☐

This illustrates a common mistake. Which box should the person whose family spends £10 or £15 tick?

QUESTIONS WHICH USE DIFFICULT WORDS OR ASSUME KNOWLEDGE

● Do you think that Britain should disarm unilaterally?

This question may produce bad answers because people do not understand the words. Always explain technical terms or difficult words.

● Do you think that the amount of money which Britain spends on foreign aid is:

About right ☐
Too much ☐
Too little ☐

This assumes that the person answering the question knows how much money is spent on aid; without this knowledge they would find the question impossible to answer. Always give people the information they need for this sort of question.

ACTIVITY >

All of the questions in the questionnaire on the next page have at least one problem. Read the questions carefully and find as many problems as you can. When you have done this, rewrite these questions without the problems. Ask someone to check your questions.

Questionnaire on video recorders

Could you please answer the following questions:
1 What is your name and address?_____

_____
2 How old are you?   Under 15☐ 15–30☐ 30–50☐ 50 or older☐
3 Sex?_____
4 What is your social class?_____
5 How long have you owned a video recorder for?_____
6 How many hours a week do you use your video for?
     5 or less   ☐
     5–15   ☐
     15–25   ☐
     25 or more. ☐
7 Do you use your video for?
    taping programmes off television   ☐ *(tick one only)*
    or watching films   ☐
8 How many pirate videos have you watched?_____
9 Where do you get pirate videos from?_____
10 Would you agree that 'video nasties' are depraved and immoral and
that people who sell them should be locked up?   Yes☐   No☐
11 Since having your video recorder is it true that you have watched more
television and gone to the cinema less often?   Yes☐
                  No☐

Thank you

ACTIVITY ▷

Now try writing some questions of your own. Choose one of the hypotheses on page 5 in Chapter 1. Write ten questions to test your hypothesis including one of each of the five types of question (classification, knowledge, factual, opinion and motivation) and use both closed coded and open questions.

1.5 Checking your questions

When you have written your questions test them on five people to see if they are easy to understand and answer (this is known as a **PILOT STUDY** and is used by researchers before carrying out their survey.) Rewrite your questions if there are any problems with them.

1.6 Writing your own questionnaire

Now write out a questionnaire for your own project.

- Make sure that all of the questions are relevant to your hypothesis.
- For each question summarise, in a few sentences, why you are asking it and what you expect to find out.
- Make sure that you order your questions logically; classification questions usually come first and knowledge questions come before attitude questions.
- Do not ask any questions by which people can be identified such as name or address. Questionnaires must always be anonymous if you want people to be honest.
- Carry out a pilot survey as before.

- After your pilot survey rewrite your questions if any of them were unclear.
- It is important that you keep all copies of your questions, including those which you have rewritten, so that you can show the stages that your research has gone through.

2 SELECTING A SAMPLE

To be fully accurate, a survey should be filled in by everyone it applies to. This would, however, take too long and cost too much. You must therefore give your questionnaires to a **SAMPLE**; this simply means asking only part of the group of people who your survey applies to.

2.1 Deciding how many people to ask

If you want to make generalisations from your survey you must ask quite a large number of people. However giving out large numbers of questionnaires can take a lot of time and can cost quite a lot of money, especially if copies are to be printed. The analysis of results is also time consuming. You must therefore not be too ambitious. Fifty questionnaires would be a good number to aim for; if time and cost make this number impossible you must complete at least twenty. Decide how many questionnaires you are going to give out before you start, rather than just giving them out until you feel that you have done enough. For analysis you might find it useful to do a number, such as twenty-five or fifty, which can be easily converted into a percentage.

2.2 Choosing a random sample

However many people you decide to give your questionnaire to it is important that your sample is **RANDOM**. This means not just people who you know since this may produce biased or one-sided results. If you are trying to find out what people think about under age drinking your friends would give you a biased set of answers since they are all likely to have the same opinions. Your sample needs to be **REPRESENTATIVE** of the group. A random sample is one where everyone has an equal chance of being included. So if your research is on fifth year students at your school you must select from all fifth year students at random. If your research is on people who live on your housing estate you must select from every house at random. This involves drawing up a **SAMPLING FRAME**. This is a list of everyone who could be included, for example, a list of all fifth year students or a list of all houses on your estate. Lists like this are often available for you to use. The school will have a central list of all students in each year for example. You then need to select your sample at random from this list. If there are two hundred houses on your estate and you want to complete twenty questionnaires you must select out every tenth house on the list. You can also select a random sample by using random number tables or sometimes by using a computer although you may need help from your teacher to use either of these methods. For small samples it is accurate enough to put all names into a hat and pick out the number that you require.

It may be that the group in which you are interested is divided into definite sub-groups, for example male and female. You will want to make sure that each sub-group is properly represented in your sample. If there are sixty girls and forty boys in your fifth year you will want to ask girls and boys in the ratio six to four; that is six girls to every four boys. If you are asking twenty people this will mean asking twelve girls and eight boys. To make sure that you got the right numbers you would take two separate samples, one of males and one of females. This is known as a **STRATIFIED SAMPLE**.

If you are asking questions in the street, you must be careful to ask people who fit your quota.

If you are asking people on the street you cannot possibly get a random sample. Therefore you must take a **QUOTA SAMPLE**. Before you go out decide what sort of people you want to interview. For example: five males under forty, five females under forty, five males over forty, five females over forty. You then ask people to fill in your questionnaire, making sure that you ask the right sorts of people to fulfil your quota.

In practice some groups may be regarded as fairly random. For example you do not need to sample primary school classes or mixed ability classes in secondary schools if you are only interested in this age range.

It is important to try to get a random sample to avoid bias in your research. You must explain, in your project, how you got your sample and any problems you experienced in selecting a random sample. If it was not possible to get a random sample say so and discuss how you think this might influence your results.

ACTIVITY

If you wanted to find out what people in Britain feel about the present government would the photo above be a good sample to ask? Explain what different types of people might be missed out. How would you go about getting a fully representative sample?

2.3 What to do about people who refuse to respond

With all surveys there is the problem of **NON RESPONSE**. People in your sample may refuse to fill in the questionnaire or forget to return it. This may make your results less accurate, especially if the people who don't reply are a certain type of person such as older people.

To get as high a response rate as possible:

- Your questionnaire must be anonymous; there must be no way in which people can be identified.
- Keep your questionnaire short so that it does not take up a lot of time to fill in.
- Either wait while people complete the questions (or write the answers in for them) or arrange a time when you can collect the questionnaires.
- Have some spare copies for people who lose or spoil their questionnaires.
- If people do refuse to answer your questions you should say so when you write up your results; discuss how this may affect your results.

3 RECORDING YOUR ANSWERS

When you have selected your sample you are ready to carry out your survey. You then need to work out a clear way of recording your answers. The easiest way to do this is to write out your questions on a single sheet and reproduce them so that you have one copy for each person to be surveyed. This may, however, prove costly and if your survey is quite simple containing mostly closed coded questions it is quite easy to record your answers on a grid as shown below. The numbers across the top represent the number of people surveyed whereas the numbers down the side refer to the questions.

PEOPLE:	1	2	3	4 $\longrightarrow$
QUESTIONS: 1	M	F	F	M
2	(b)	(c)	(b)	(a)
3 $\downarrow$				

If each alternative response to your questions is given a letter you can then ask people the questions and write down the answers.
For example:

1 Are you (a) male ☐ or (b) female ☐
2 How old are you? (a) under 16 ☐ (b) 16–40 ☐ (c) 41 + ☐

For open questions you need to leave more space and write the answers in.

4 ANALYSING YOUR RESULTS

Take each question and summarise your results. For closed coded questions this will involve counting up answers and drawing tables and graphs. For open questions it will involve seeing what sort of things people have said. Do any answers come up several times? You should copy out some of the answers and comment on them; were these the answers you expected? Do different people have different opinions etc.?

4.1 Analysing closed coded questions

First draw up a **TALLY** of answers. This may look like this:

Question

Is there too much	☐
too little	☐
the right amount	☐ (of sport on television?)

Results

Too much	ЖТ	ЖТ	ЖТ	IIII	24
Too little	ЖТ	IIII			9
About right	ЖТ	ЖТ	ЖТ	II	17
Total number of people					50

This result should be summarised in words and can also be shown on a graph, pie chart or pictogram. A pictogram would look like this:

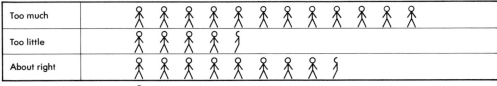

Too much	𝕏 𝕏 𝕏 𝕏 𝕏 𝕏 𝕏 𝕏 𝕏 𝕏 𝕏 𝕏
Too little	𝕏 𝕏 𝕏 ⸝
About right	𝕏 𝕏 𝕏 𝕏 𝕏 𝕏 𝕏 ⸝

𝕏 Represents two people

In an earlier hypothesis it was suggested that females were more likely than males to feel that there was too much sport on television. We can find out if this was right by **CROSS ANALYSIS**. Do a tally as before, but this time record male and female answers in different columns:

	Female	Male	Total
Too much	8	16	24
Too little	6	3	9
About right	12	5	17
Total	26	24	50

From this table we must conclude that the hypothesis was wrong and that females are happier about the amount of sport on television than males.

It was also expected that people involved in sport would be less unhappy about the amount of sport on television than people who were not involved. Again we can see if this was right by cross analysis; we have to recount the number of people giving different answers, classifying them this time not by sex but by the way they answered a question on whether they took part in sport themselves.

	Involved in sport	Not involved in sport	Total
Too much	2	22	24
Too little	9	–	9
About right	15	2	17
Total	26	24	50

From the results we can argue that the hypothesis was right.

For your survey you can:

- Count up the different answers to each question separately and summarise your findings. Were your results what you expected?
- Wherever possible cross analyse questions so that you can see what sorts of people have different opinions.

One important area of cross analysis is to see if people who score high on knowledge questions have different attitudes from people who get knowledge questions wrong. For example on a survey on vivisection (using animals for experiments) on which there were three knowledge questions the following results might be obtained:

Question

Do you feel that animal experiments should be controlled more strictly than they are at present?

Yes ☐
No ☐

Result   Yes: 26   No: 24   Total: 50

Results on knowledge questions:

Number of people getting two or three knowledge questions right	30
Number of people getting one or less knowledge questions right	20
Total number of people asked	50

Cross analysis: Do people with more knowledge have different attitudes from those with less knowledge?

		High knowledge score	Low knowledge score	Total
Need more control:	Yes	24	2	26
	No	6	18	24
	Total	30	20	50

This shows that people who know more on the topic are more likely to think that experiments need to be controlled.

4.2 Concluding your survey

After analysing every question and carrying out any cross analysis you should summarise your main research findings. If you looked at any other studies in your background research discuss whether your results were the same, if not, can you offer any explanations for the differences? Comment fully on whether your hypothesis was correct or not; were you surprised by any of the results? Why? How successful do you think that your questionnaire was? Did you have any particular problems such as getting a random sample or questions which were misunderstood? If you were to carry out this research again would you make any changes?

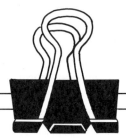

CHECKLIST

- Make sure that you have written fully about every stage of your research as set out in the different sections of this chapter.

- Describe your background research in detail

- Include a copy not just of your final questionnaire, but also any early plans. If your pilot study caused you to rewrite any questions — explain why. For your final questionnaire explain why you asked each question: what was each designed to find out?

- Explain how you got your sample and any problems which you had.

- Analyse your survey in detail and relate your findings back to your main research question or hypothesis.

- Outline any problems with your research and explain how these might have influenced your results.

Chapter Three
Interviewing People

An interview is simply a conversation between two people when one, the interviewer, asks questions of the other, the interviewee. Interviews may be used in your enquiry in several different ways.

1 DIFFERENT TYPES OF INTERVIEWS

1.1 Structured or formal interviews

You can use STRUCTURED or FORMAL INTERVIEWS to read out questions from a questionnaire. This may produce better results than if people fill in their own answers because you can explain any questions which the interviewee does not understand and you can make sure that all the questions are answered properly. However, interviews take a long time to carry out. If your questions are mostly closed-coded a questionnaire might be easier. If you do intend to use an interview in this way you should be careful how you write the questions. The only other thing you need to decide is how you are going to record your answers. Section 2.4 below gives some advice on this.

> CHAPTER 2

1.2 Unstructured or informal interviews

For UNSTRUCTURED or INFORMAL INTERVIEWS you will not have a list of closed coded questions. Your questions will be far more open and the interviewee will be given time to talk at length about his or her experiences and opinions rather than just choosing from different answers. You are most likely to use this type of interview if you want detailed information and opinions rather than just facts and figures, or if you do not know enough to list all of the possible alternative answers. This type of interview is more flexible than a formal interview; you can reword questions to make sure that they are understood, you can suggest different ideas if people dry up and you can, at times, ignore your questions and follow up other interesting ideas which come up in discussion. Because your questions are not closed coded this sort of interview will be much more difficult to analyse than a questionnaire or formal interview. Also, because it is time consuming, you are unlikely to be able to carry out as many interviews of this type as you would using a questionnaire or formal interview.

1.3 Interviewing 'experts'

You may wish to use the interview method to get the opinions of one person who you think is important rather than a general view from several people. This person may be a doctor, headteacher, marriage guidance counsellor, police inspector, local Member of Parliament or any other person with specialised knowledge. A specific case when you might use this type of interview would be if you were carrying out oral history research. You could find out about an historical period by interviewing someone who lived at that time. Although this interview will be a 'one-off' it will need careful preparation as for the other types of interview.

2 PREPARING FOR YOUR INTERVIEW(S)

Since formal interviews are very similar to questionnaires the rest of this chapter concentrates on the second and third types of interview. Before you can actually carry out your interview you need to do a lot of planning; this is shown below:

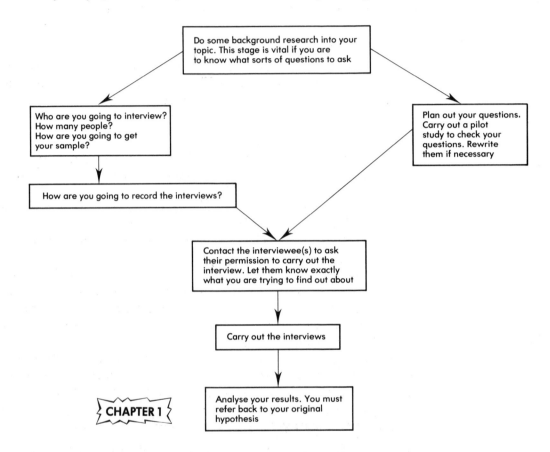

Do some background research into your topic. This stage is vital if you are to know what sorts of questions to ask

Who are you going to interview?
How many people?
How are you going to get your sample?

Plan out your questions. Carry out a pilot study to check your questions. Rewrite them if necessary

How are you going to record the interviews?

Contact the interviewee(s) to ask their permission to carry out the interview. Let them know exactly what you are trying to find out about

Carry out the interviews

CHAPTER 1

Analyse your results. You must refer back to your original hypothesis

2.1 Background research

CHAPTER 5

CHAPTER 8

Before planning your interviews you must do some background research. This will involve reading books and leaflets and talking to people who may know something about your topic. It might also involve writing off for general information or looking at research which other people have done on the topic. For example, if you were going to interview married couples about how they share jobs in the home it would help if you observed your own family, talked informally to your parents and friends, and looked at some of the research which sociologists have done on this topic. This would help you to ask questions which were relevant.

2.2 Who are you going to interview?

If you are carrying out several informal interviews you must first decide how many you can handle. Be careful not to be too adventurous; informal interviews not only take a long time to carry out, they take even longer to analyse and it is better to do a small number well than a large number badly. You are unlikely to be able to

CHAPTER 2

carry out more than ten and even this might be too many. Second you must decide who to interview. As for questionnaires, your sample should be as random as possible. If you are unable to gain a random sample you must say so and explain how this might bias your results.

If you are interviewing an expert this stage doesn't represent a problem since there is usually only one person who you can interview.

2.3 Preparing your questions

It would be helpful if you read Chapter 2 (sections 1.2, 1.3, 1.4) on different types of questions and problems to avoid before writing your questions. Although you are likely to ask some closed questions most of your questions for both types of interview will be open. Planning your interview questions involves four stages which you should follow carefully:

- You should first write any classification questions (age, sex etc.) or basic factual questions which are relevant to your hypothesis. These questions are likely to be closed.
- List the general areas that you want to talk about in your interview. For each general area write a very open question which covers what you want to find out. It should be impossible to answer this question with a 'yes' or 'no' or with any single word.
- Underneath each open question write as many related questions as you can think of. Again these should not be answerable with a single word. These questions should cover areas that you hope the interviewee will discuss in answer to your open question but which you can ask if he/she dries up or misses the point.
- If possible try your questions out on someone to see if they work. For interviewing an expert this may be difficult but at least get someone to go through your questions with you. You may have to rewrite some of your questions to make them clearer. It would be useful if you taped this practice interview to gain experience of using a tape recorder.

The separate stages are worked through in the examples below:

EXAMPLE: INTERVIEWING AN EXPERT

Research question: How important is religion in Britain today?
Interviewee: Local vicar.
Background questions: Size of parish, number and type (age, sex etc.) of regular congregation.
Main areas to cover:
- Falling church attendance.
- Use of the church for births, marriages and deaths.
- The church and young people.
- The role of the church in politics.
- The importance of religious education in schools.

General question: What do you feel are the reasons for fewer people attending church today than, say, fifty years ago?

In 1985, less than 50 per cent of marriages took place in church

Related questions:
- Is the church less relevant to people's lives today?
- Is the church out-dated, not keeping up with change in society?
- What about the growth of other things for people, especially young people, to do — how has this affected church attendance?
- Why do people go to church? Religious reasons, social reasons, pressures from other people, 'respectability' or 'status'? Have these reasons changed at all in the last fifty years?
- How do you feel that the church should respond to declining church attendances?

EXAMPLE: INFORMAL INTERVIEWS

Research question: How equal are marriages today?
Interviewee: Married woman.
Background questions: Ages of couple, number and ages of children, hours worked outside the home by husband and wife.
Main areas to cover:

- Housework
- Childcare
- Decision making — including who decides how to spend the family income
- Leisure or spare-time activities

General question:
How do you and your husband share out work in the home, including jobs like decorating and gardening as well as cleaning and washing etc?
Related questions:
- Are there any jobs which are definitely yours and definitely his?
- How often does he do/how often do you do ..... (use a list of jobs given in her answer or provide your own.)
- When your husband does jobs in the home (pick up examples from her answer to the general question) do you have to ask him or does he do it voluntarily?
- Are you happy with the way you share jobs in the home — are there any changes you would like to make?

EXAMPLE: AN ORAL HISTORY INTERVIEW

Research question: What was life like in Britain during the Second World War?
Interviewee: Woman, aged seventy.
Background questions: Age of interviewee during the war, status of interviewee during the war (married or single, children or not, etc.) Occupation at the time, if any.

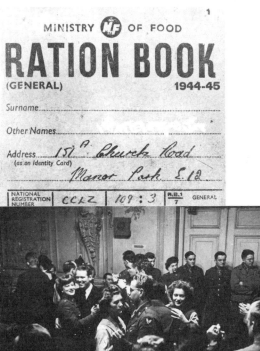

Main areas to cover:

- Rationing
- Blackout
- Women working
- Evacuees
- Entertainment
- Sources of information

General question:
How did rationing affect the sort of meals that you ate?
Related questions:

- What were the basic rations?
- Was there any food which was not available at all?
- What were your typical meals?
- Can you remember how you had to change any recipes because you couldn't get the ingredients?
- How important was the Black Market to you in getting food?

ACTIVITY

Choose one from the research questions listed below and go through the four stages as in the above examples. You must first decide who the interviewee would be. Discuss your questions with someone when you have finished to check that they cannot be answered with a single word.

- Do private schools provide a better education than state schools?
- Is the Youth Training Scheme worth keeping?
- What are the causes of football violence? How can it be reduced?
- What are the effects of long term unemployment?
- What is the role of the local newspaper in the community?
- What differences are there in the education of boys and girls?

ACTIVITY

You should now be ready to prepare your own interview questions. When you have written out the whole interview ask someone to play the part of the interviewee and try it out. You may then need to rewrite some of your questions.

2.4 Recording the interview

Before you can carry out your interview you must decide how you are going to record the information. You must not rely on memory since you are likely to forget some of the interview and you might put your own interpretation on what you have heard. You therefore have two choices:

You can write down the answers. There are several problems with this. You may not be able to write quickly enough to get everything down. If this is so you will have to concentrate on getting down the main points; it is helpful if you develop your own system of shorthand so that you do not have to write everything out in full. Another difficulty is that you may be so busy trying to write everything down that you lose track of the questions. If informal interviews are to be flexible you need to be able to guide the conversation rather than just asking a list of questions. If you do have to write answers down it might be easier if you stick quite closely to your questions. A final problem is that some interviewees might be put off by your writing.

You could tape record the interview. If you have a good portable cassette recorder and the person being interviewed agrees, this is by far the best method since it overcomes the problems of writing. If you do intend to tape your interview(s) it is important that you have a good tape recorder, and know how to use it. Practice working with it beforehand, not just using the switches but speaking clearly. You must have a tape which is long enough for the whole interview because changing tapes in the middle of an interview can be very off-putting. If an interviewee refuses to let you tape the interview or even to take notes, you will have to rely on memory. In this case you must write quick notes on the interview as soon as possible after it has ended.

2.5 Arranging the interview

You should now be ready to carry out your interview(s). Contact your interviewee(s) well in advance either by letter, by telephone, or in person. Make sure that you tell them:

CHAPTER 5

- who you are and what you are doing your research on. You might also tell them the general areas that you are interested in and why you have chosen to interview them.
- how long (roughly) the interview will last
- how you would like to record the interview
- what times would be most convenient to you and
- that their answers will be confidential and that you will not use their names in your project. This last point does not apply to the 'expert'.

If any of your chosen interviewees refuse to be interviewed you should try to replace them with someone else and state in your project that you had to do this.

2.6 Carrying out the interviews

If you have prepared your interview properly actually carrying it out should be quite straightforward. The following are a few points which you should bear in mind.

- Arrive on time and have everything you need with you.
- Some interviewees might be nervous especially if they are being taped; help them to relax by being friendly and relaxed yourself.
- Explain generally what you are going to ask them before you start the interview; there is no need to record this.
- Be careful to avoid the problem of interviewer bias. Avoid giving your own opinions and try not to give away your feelings by your tone of voice, the expression on your face or the way in which you word your questions. Some interviewees might subconsciously alter their answers if they feel that there is a 'right' or 'expected' answer.
- When asking your questions be flexible; as long as you cover all of your areas it doesn't matter if they are in a different order from your questions. Also if your interviewee discusses an issue which isn't in your questions, but is important, allow them to continue. Your questions are meant to help you, not to be absolutely followed. If you feel that a question has not been answered fully, or if your interviewee dries up or gets confused, ask other simpler questions; you should have prepared these just in case you need them. On the other hand don't worry if you don't have to ask many of your questions to get the information that you need.
- When you have finished your interview don't forget to thank the interviewee for their time and co-operation.

2.7 Analysing your results

It is not enough to carry out interviews and write them up; you must use your findings to answer your research questions. So long as you include the tape(s) in your project there is no need to transcribe (copy out) all of your interview(s). If you do want to write out the whole interview — and you may wish to do this if it is just one interview — you still need to write about it and comment on the answers. The important thing in analysing an interview is to refer back to your research questions or hypothesis.

Whereas with a questionnaire the main aim is to draw up tables of statistics, an interview is more concerned with getting detailed information. Because of this, most of your analysis will be descriptive.

Your analysis will be different depending on whether you have done one interview or several. General points to consider in each case are given below.

2.8 Analysing interviews with experts and oral history interviews

Both of these sorts of interview will probably just be a small part of a project which uses other methods of enquiry as well. Since in both cases you have only done one interview it will not be possible to draw up tables of statistics, and your account will be descriptive.

- Write an account of the background to the interview including why you chose this person, what exactly you wanted to find out about and how this fits in with your enquiry as a whole. Include also copies of any letters sent and received.
- Write out your questions, possibly explaining why you thought these questions were relevant.
- Listen carefully to the tape and make notes; write out in full any passages which are particularly interesting or are important to your hypothesis.
- Summarise the interview briefly, picking out any important points and commenting on these in more detail. If you choose to transcribe the interview you must still underline any important passages and discuss these after the transcript. What exactly have you learnt from this interview? Make sure that you relate your findings back to the research questions or hypothesis that you began with.
- Comment on how you think the interview went. Did you have any problems in carrying it out? How happy are you with your results? If you were to do this work again would you improve it in any way?
- You may need to refer to the interview again in your general conclusion at the end of your project or in other sections.

2.9 Analysing informal interviews

Informal interviews may be used alongside other methods of research as part of an enquiry, or they may be the only or main method or research used in your enquiry. Because you are carrying out more than one interview it may be possible to draw up some simple statistics on basic points such as the number of hours spent on housework by men or women each week. Generally however, because the questions are open and likely to be answered in different ways by each interviewee, statistics will be rare and most of your analysis will be descriptive.

- Write out in full the background to the research. This could include:
- reference to research which has been done on this topic before,
- reference to your own experience and informal observations,
- your overall hypothesis,
- why you chose to use informal interviews rather than any other research methods,
- the interview questions with some explanation for why these questions were thought to be important,
- information on how you chose your interviewees; what sort of people did you want to interview, whether your sample was random, how your results might have been influenced and
- copies of any letters sent or received.
- Listen carefully to the tapes and take notes on them, write out in full any passages which are particularly interesting.
- Summarise the interviews and use the information to discuss your research questions.

This last stage of analysis is quite difficult because each interviewee might have given totally different answers to your questions yet you need to try to compare them. There are several ways in which you can carry out this analysis. Perhaps the best solution would be to first summarise each interview separately, including any interesting quotations and picking out the points which are most important to the hypothesis. Then, to compare the interviews, set a list of key questions. Some of these questions would be quite simple, others more complicated, trying to link different areas. An example is shown.

EXAMPLE: HOW EQUAL ARE MARRIAGES IN MODERN BRITAIN?

- How equal were the marriages in terms of sharing housework? Did men do an equal share or did they just 'help' their wives with a few jobs each week?
- How satisfied were women with the amount of housework that their husbands did?
- Did men who did most housework also share childcare, decision making or leisure?
- Were the women who were most dissatisfied with the amount of housework done, those women whose husbands actually did least?

It might be possible to carry out the analysis without summarising each interview separately, but this may be quite difficult to do.

Getting back to the general analysis of interviews there are three more important stages:

- If you started by looking at research done by other people on your topic, how do your results compare? If they are different, why do you think this is?
- Draw some general conclusions from your research. What are the main things you have learnt from it? Was your hypothesis right?
- Comment on the interviews themselves. How do you think they went? Did you have any particular problems? Did you feel that you influenced the interviewees in any way? If you were to do this research again, how would you improve it?

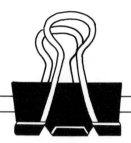

CHECKLIST

- Carry out some background research into your topic. Don't forget to write this up as well as the interview itself.

- Decide who you want to interview — what sort of people and how many?

- Write to your interviewee(s) as soon as you have a clear idea of what you actually want to do. Allow plenty of time to arrange interviews.

- Prepare your questions carefully using your background research. Try your questions out, if possible, by doing a practice interview.

- Before carrying out your interview(s) make sure that you know how to use a tape recorder; check that your machine works.

- After the interview(s) analyse your results carefully. It isn't enough just to do interviews; you must write about what you have learnt and how this fits in with your hypothesis.

- Discuss any problems that you had in doing the research.

Chapter Four
Observing People and Groups

We are all involved in many situations every day – yet how much do we observe? Often we are so used to what goes on that we take it for granted. We would not be able to describe fully what happens to an outsider. Using **OBSERVATION** as a method of research involves you in looking closely at a situation to discover what actually happens.

1 WHY USE OBSERVATION?

There are two situations in which you might use observation as a method of research.

1.1 Observation as background research

If you are studying a group which you know nothing about, such as a factory or a playgroup, you could do a short piece of observation at the beginning of your project to help you get ideas and to help you to write your hypothesis. You could then test this hypothesis using other methods such as questionnaires.

1.2 Observation as your main method of enquiry

Alternatively you could use observation as your main method of research and it is this that the rest of this chapter discusses. Whereas surveys are useful if you want to find out facts and figures, observation is useful if you want to understand in detail how people behave. Some things are difficult to study using surveys, not so much because people tell lies, but because we don't always realise how we behave.

For example, many people who say that they are not superstitious automatically walk round ladders, students who have done observations in my lessons have shown that I spend more time helping male students than female students although it is something which I always try to avoid, and in families which would claim to have shared roles women may still be observed to take overall responsibility.

Observation is therefore very useful for finding out what actually happens. It is also useful for discovering the unwritten rules which govern a situation. These unwritten rules or **NORMS** can be illustrated by a simple example. If you stand in a long queue (to buy tickets or for a large summer sale) you will notice that people observe certain rules, for example:

- Pushing in is generally not expected or 'allowed'.
- Queues are fairly orderly, straight lines rather than a loose crowd.
- You must stay in your place. You cannot arrive to mark your place and then go away, although other queuers will normally accept it if you go away just for a few minutes. Observers of queues have noticed that when people have gone away for a long time they have not been allowed back in their places.

- You can't generally save places for more people although you can queue for someone else.
- In some cases a 'blind eye' is turned to people pushing in but this often depends on the type of person involved.

Observation in other countries may show that these norms do not operate in the same way.

ACTIVITY

Spend a brief period of time actually observing in a situation in which you normally participate, such as in a classroom, at a meeting, with the family, at a youth club or with a group of friends. Write down the unwritten rules of behaviour. Discuss these with another participant of the group, have you missed anything out?

2 TYPES OF OBSERVATION

In practice all observation involves some participation. The observer is involved in some way with the group he/she is observing. However, the degree of involvement can vary and it is useful for us to divide observation into two types.

2.1 Participant observation

You can observe in a situation which you are actually part of such as a classroom, a youth club or a work experience. This may be a group which you already belong to or it may be one which you become part of in order to do the observation. Generally speaking it is better to join a group to observe it rather than observe a group to which you already belong. The main reason for this is that it would be very difficult for you to observe your own family for example; you would probably not notice a lot of what goes on because you are so used to it that you take it for granted. It would also be difficult in this situation for you to remain objective or unbiased in your research.

2.2 Direct or non-participant observation

You can alternatively observe in a situation in which you are not fully involved, where people know that you are an outsider observing them. You could do this sort of observation in a classroom, in a meeting, in the law courts, accompanying a police officer, in a supermarket or in a library for example.

3 PROBLEMS WITH OBSERVATION

Although observation can provide information which is detailed and which cannot be got in any other way there are problems which you need to try to avoid. Below are the main problems which you might have.

Some groups would be very difficult to observe. They may be limited to certain ages or sexes or, as in the case of the Moonies—photographed above—may not accept outsiders

- Getting accepted by a group to observe can sometimes be a problem especially for participant observation.
- Participant observation may be covert or overt. In **COVERT PARTICIPANT OBSERVATION** those being observed do not know that you are studying them; they think that you are an ordinary member of the group. This raises the moral or ethical problem of whether it is acceptable to 'spy' on people in this way. In **OVERT PARTICIPANT OBSERVATION** and in direct observation the participants know that they are being observed. You need to consider whether this might cause them to act differently.
- If you become fully involved in the group you may become a poor observer in that you might begin to take things for granted and not notice them. You could also yourself change the behaviour of the group if, for example, you became involved in making the decisions.
- When carrying out participant observation you will have a problem of recording your observations. You will have to rely on your memory until you are away from the group.
- For all observation, what we see and how we interpret it depends to some extent on our own values. You must constantly try to look at the situation from different sides.

Many of these problems cannot be totally avoided but you must be aware of them and must try to judge how much they have affected your findings.

4 CARRYING OUT YOUR RESEARCH

Whether you are doing participant or direct observation there are three stages to your research. These are getting into the group, structuring the observation and recording the data, and analysing the results. The problems you face in each case will depend to some extent on the type of observation you are doing.

4.1 Getting into the group

For participant observation this might be the most difficult stage of your research. If you are studying a group which you already belong to 'getting in' obviously is not a problem (although there are other problems with studying people who you know well which have already been discussed). If you intend to join a group in order to observe them it would be useful if you had a contact who could introduce you. You also need to learn the norms of the group so that you can fit in easily. The number of groups which you can observe in this way will clearly be limited because of your age. For some groups, such as youth clubs of which you are not already a member, and sports clubs, there may be no problem of acceptance. For other groups, such as a teenage gang or a specialist club, it might be more difficult.

Because of this and other problems with participant observation, many students prefer to use non-participant observation where getting into the group is easier. When you have decided what sort of group you wish to study you must ask their permission. If it is a class in your own school which you wish to observe you must simply ask the teacher. Be careful not to simply choose a teacher whom you like or know well; you should try to choose your teacher at random. If you wish to observe in another institution such as a primary school, a hospital or the law courts you should write to them explaining who you are and what you want to do. If your chosen group refuses to let you observe then you must simply try an alternative.

CHAPTER 5

Some situations such as open public meetings will not need arranging in this way since you can simply attend. Unless it is absolutely necessary in order to gain entry, do not say exactly what hypothesis you are testing since if they know this, the people being observed might subconsciously change their behaviour.

Having gained entry you must decide for how long you are going to observe. This should be a reasonable length of time, enough to get an overall picture. For example half of a meeting or part of a lesson could give you an inaccurate idea on whether males or females dominate; you must stay for at least the whole meeting or whole lesson. For participant observation you must stay with the group for long enough to learn their norms. Ideally this should be several months but clearly this will not be possible; you should however stay for as long as your time scale allows.

4.2 Structuring your observation and recording the data

If your observation is to be useful you must have a reasonable idea for what you are searching beforehand. Structuring your observation in advance is most important for **DIRECT OBSERVATION**. For this type of research it is sometimes helpful to do a trial piece of observation beforehand when you just sit and watch to gain ideas which you can then look at more systematically in your proper observation. It may be helpful, after a practice observation, to draw up a grid on which to record your observations — this helps you to be more objective. How structured your grid is will depend upon what you are observing as shown by the examples below.

EXAMPLE: OBSERVATION IN A HUMANITIES CLASSROOM

Research question: Do teachers pay equal attention to male and female students?
*Sex of teacher*_____
No. of students: Male_____   Female_____
*Length of observation:*_____
Teacher activities: *Time:*

- Talking to the whole class   5 mins   2 mins   50 seconds etc.
- Completing own work/students working —
- Talking to male student(s)   10 seconds   2 mins   3 mins   etc.
- Talking to female student(s)   2 mins   30 seconds   50 seconds etc.
- In whole class discussion   —

Number of questions asked of male students: IIII III

Number of questions asked of female students: IIII   IIII   I I

EXAMPLE: OBSERVATION IN THE MAGISTRATES COURT

Research question: Does the sentence depend on the crime committed or are
other factors relevant?
Record sheet for each case:
*Crime:*_____
*Age of offender:*_____
*Sex of offender:*_____

Job of offender:_____
General appearance and manner in court:_____
_____
Previous record:_____
Special circumstances:_____
_____
Sentence:_____
Comments:_____
_____

EXAMPLE: OBSERVATION IN A LOCAL COUNCIL MEETING

Research question: Who dominates in making decisions?
This observation would take place without a grid; rather general notes would be taken on the meeting, noting who speaks, what decisions are made etc.

ACTIVITY

Select one of the following situations, write a research question and draw up a framework for direct observation to answer your question.

- A tutor group
- A primary school classroom
- A supermarket checkout
- A job centre
- A doctor's waiting room
- A restaurant
- A queue

For **PARTICIPANT OBSERVATION** it is important that you do not structure your research too much in advance. This could cause you to miss important points. You should have some general questions in mind that you would like to answer; these might change as your observation continues and you come to understand the situation more fully.

EXAMPLE: PARTICIPANT OBSERVATION IN A WORKPLACE
This may be a Saturday job or work experience.

Research question: What are the formal and informal (unwritten) rules of the workplace? Participant observation to discover the informal rules.

General questions:

1 How much work do people actually do during the working day?

- How long do people take for tea breaks?
- Do workers take other breaks during the day?
- At what time do workers actually start working at the beginning of the day and stop working at the end of the day?
- What different ways are used for avoiding work?
- Do all people have the same approach?

2 What is the informal structure of the workplace?

- Do people have different roles to perform?
- Are there members of the workplace who do not fulfil their roles?
- How do other people cope with this?
- Do people work together or on their own?
- Do people cover for each other?
- Who makes the decisions on day to day matters?
- Are there any clear cliques or sub-groups in the workplace?

3 Do workers cut any corners to get their work done? (For example overloading a supermarket trolley with goods to avoid a return journey or ignoring health and safety regulations.)

For participant observation a big problem at this stage will be recording your information. You will have to rely on memory a great deal so you must write things down as soon as possible, preferably as soon as you get home from your observation. Some participant observers also carry a small notebook around with them and jot things down whenever they have the opportunity.

At the end of your participant observation period you should have a lengthy set of notes which might include rough quotations but are likely to be more descriptive. These notes might take the form of an observation diary.

5 ANALYSING YOUR RESULTS

If you have planned your observation carefully, analysing your results should not be too difficult. For direct observation you may produce some tables and graphs, but for both types of observation most of your analysis will be descriptive. It is important that you do not just describe what you saw or just include your observation diary. You must order your observations so that you can make general points about the group which you observed. You should illustrate these points with actual examples wherever possible. The aim of your analysis is either to answer the questions which you set yourself at the beginning or to test your hypothesis.

For the observation on a workplace the analysis would involve going through notes and organising them to answer the questions illustrating general points with examples wherever possible. In a conclusion a comparison could be made between the informal structure which had been observed with the formal structure.

For the observation on the magistrates court the analysis would involve grouping the cases that had been observed so that it could be seen if people who committed the same offence gained a similar sentence or whether people committing more serious offences always got stiffer sentences. If the sentence did not always fit the crime, other factors such as age, class, or past record could be looked at. Then this would be written up with examples to illustrate, followed-up, perhaps by an interview with a magistrate. If you have not pre-structured your observation in any way your analysis will be much more difficult. You must read through your notes carefully to find any patterns. It is then useful if you set a series of questions which you can answer using your observation.

Finally, having discussed your findings, you must discuss your observation itself. Did you experience any problems? How might these have influenced your findings? Did you have to change your research questions half way through the research? If you were to carry out this research again how would you do it differently?

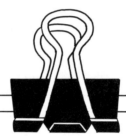

CHECKLIST

- What were your general research questions or your hypothesis?

- Describe any background research that you did. This could include any informal observation which you did to get ideas.

- Explain why you are using observation rather than any other method to test your hypothesis. Did you expect any problems? If so how did you attempt to overcome them?

- Where did you plan to observe and why?

- Describe the observation itself. How did you get accepted, how long did you observe for, how did you structure your observation?

- Include your observation diary or observation sheets.

- Analyse your results and relate your findings back to your main research question or hypothesis.

- Outline any problems with your research, how you attempted to overcome them and how these might have influenced your results.

Chapter Five
Writing Letters

1 WHAT SORT OF LETTER TO WRITE

There are three sorts of situation in which you might write a letter to help you get information for your project.

- *To a person or organisation* asking them if you can visit to carry out an interview or to observe what they do. For example, you may write to your local police station, to a local Job Centre, to a Probation Officer or to a local factory.
- *To an organisation or pressure group* asking them to send you any printed information which they have available, or for references to books which you could use. For example, you may write to pressure groups for and against abortion or vivisection, to the Commission for Racial Equality, to Shelter, to the Campaign for Nuclear Disarmament or to the Child Poverty Action group. This sort of letter might be written quite early in your project while you are still sorting out your ideas.
- *To an 'expert', an organisation, local authority or someone who has specialised knowledge on your subject* asking them to answer a series of questions. This might be similar to a questionnaire but only sent to one or a small number of people. For example, you may write to your local Member of Parliament, to the local council or to any organisation which is relevant to your hypothesis. You may use this type of letter when the person cannot be interviewed because they live too far away. This type of letter is usually written when you have done quite a lot of background work on your project and have very clear ideas about what you want to ask.

> CHAPTER 2

Often it may be necessary to combine the last two types of letter, asking for printed material and answers to specific questions.

Before you can write any kind of letter you must have a very clear idea of what exactly you want to find out and why this person or organisation might be helpful. If you write an unclear and vague letter you are likely to receive a reply which is not very useful.

2 HOW TO SET OUT A LETTER AND WHAT TO INCLUDE

How you write your letter will depend on the information you need. There are, however, certain basic rules which you should follow for all letters. These are shown in the example on the next page.

EXAMPLE:
ARRANGING A VISIT

Clearly write your own address ———→

14 Highbury Avenue
West Norton
Chesterton
C13 6ZY

Name and address of person you are writing to ———→

The Headmistress
West Norton Infants School
London Road
West Norton
Chesterton

7 October 19--

Dear Mrs Jones

State clearly who you are and your reason for writing the letter ———→

I am a fifth year student at West Norton Comprehensive.
As part of my GCSE course in Social Science I am required
to carry out an individual enquiry. I have chosen to
look at television viewing patterns of small children,
I am particularly interested to find out how much
television and what sort of programmes small children
watch and how this varies depending on for example sex
and social class. I should like to be able to
interview twenty children (ten boys and ten girls)
between the ages of 6 and 7 in order to gain answers
to these questions. Each interview should not last for
more than five minutes and could take place in the
normal classroom. I have prepared a list of interview
questions which you may see in advance if this is
necessary.

Explain what you want to do. Do you have any questions to be answered? ———→

If you are arranging a visit, list convenient times for you ———→

Would it be possible for me to visit your school within
the next three weeks to carry out these interviews?
The most convenient times for me would be either a
Monday morning (9.30 a.m. – 11 a.m.) or a Thursday
afternoon (1.30 plm. – 3.30 p.m.). However, any
alternative time would be possible.

Include a stamped addressed envelope for the reply ———→

I enclose a Stamped Addressed Envelope for your reply.

Yours sincerely

John Anderson

John Anderson

3 HOW TO USE THE INFORMATION FROM YOUR LETTER

The key word here is 'use'. It is not enough just to write letters. You need to write about the information received. What you do with the information received in reply to letters will depend upon the type of letter.

If you are writing just to arrange a visit it is enough to include copies of the letters in your project. The analysis will follow the actual visit and not the letter.

If you are writing to a pressure group or organisation for general information you may receive a large quantity of leaflets, many of which are not relevant to your hypothesis. You must select the relevant material and pass the rest on to your teacher; someone else may find it useful. Having selected information which is relevant you must write about it; it is not enough just to include it. There is often a temptation to put everything in and leave the teacher to work out why it is there. You should only put printed material such as leaflets into your project if they say something important. You should point out what this is. Be careful not to copy information out from leaflets.

Generally speaking, when using leaflets, you can include the whole leaflet if you also write about it and, perhaps, underline the most important points. You can use information from leaflets if you put it into your own words and you can cut out parts of leaflets such as photographs and tables and write about them. An example of how you could use information from leaflets is shown below. When using leaflets from pressure groups, remember that they are always one-sided and will only contain information which supports their arguments. You must therefore make every effort to present the other side of the argument. For many issues there are pressure groups representing both sides of the argument. For example whereas the Anti-Vivisection Society argues against the use of animals for experiments, the Research Defence Society argues for animal experimentation. In these cases you could use pressure group information to discuss the basic issues as background to your project.

If you are writing to an 'expert' asking set questions you need to include the reply and discuss it. Your analysis in this case should follow the guidelines set for interviewing an expert.

CHAPTER 3

Whatever sort of letter you write, remember to include a copy of both your letter and the reply in your project. The extract from a student's project on the next page shows one way in which you can use information from pressure groups.

ARE ANIMAL EXPERIMENTS NECESSARY FOR MEDICAL RESEARCH?

This is a question which is very difficult to answer. The Research Defence Society gives a lot of examples of cases where research on animals has helped provide medicines which have saved human lives. One example is discussed in the leaflet on diabetes here. It seems unlikely that treatment for diabetes would have been

developed without animal experiments. However, not all tests carried out on animals are this useful. Some drugs such as Opren and Eraldin were thought to be safe after tests on animals but have since been withdrawn because of their side effects on humans. These drugs are discussed in a leaflet produced by the Lord Dowding Fund for humane research.

What is diabetes?

In diabetes, there is a breakdown in the normal insulin activity of the body. This means that blood sugar levels become high and distorted and over a period there may be a rapid loss of flesh and large amounts of sugar are excreted in the urine as the body eliminates the excess.

Diabetes also has insidious effects which, if not controlled, can lead to other problems. Amongst these it can affect:–

The eyes–it may cause blindness;

The kidneys–it may lead to kidney failure;

The nerves–it may give rise to pain, weakness and even loss of sensation in the legs;

Heart and blood vessels–and there may be accelerated ageing of large and small blood vessels.

Further, if a diabetic becomes ill because of other diseases, his need for insulin may increase. *He may then have to use additional prescribed medicines; these would have been tested on animals.* Thus it can be seen that the diabetic patient is doubly dependent on medicinal products which have been so tested.

It is a fact that the solutions to some of the problems posed by diabetes *can only be achieved by animal experiments,* by studying the effect of diabetes on various organs, such as the kidneys and on the general metabolism of the animals.

Source: *Diabetes Research Triumph*, publ. by The Research Defence Society

OPREN'S DEMISE

The main UK post-marketing surveillance scheme uses a yellow card system to notify the government's drug watchdog (the Committee for Safety of Medicines) of adverse effects. Unfortunately the yellow card system only reveals 1-10% of side effects and was shown to be inadequate as long ago as 1976 by the drug Eraldin. Marketed by ICI for the treatment of heart conditions, Eraldin was prescribed for over 4 years before it was discovered that the drug caused serious eye problems, including blindness. The side effect had not been found in laboratory animals.

Post-marketing surveillance systems are under closer scrutiny as a result of the Opren scandal. Marketed by Eli Lilly for the treatment of arthritis, Opren belongs to a class known as Non-Steriodal Anti-Inflammatory Drugs (NSAID). In Britain there are 23 NSAIDs all competing for a slice of the £100 million market in anti-arthritis pills. Since they are very similar they are known as "me-too" drugs and whilst they can relieve the pain and inflammation associated with the disease they cannot provide a cure. However, Opren was aggressively promoted, both through the medical profession and the press, as having the potential to *cure* the disease — a compelling selling point. But the company's hopes were based on successful cures of artificially induced arthritis in rats. Human patients, it turned out, did not react the same.

The deaths caused by Opren in elderly patients arose because of their inability to metabolise the drug quickly enough and to delays in reacting to the evidence. These differences in metabolism between different age groups cannot be predicted by animal experiments (differences in metabolism between species are the rule rather than the exception) and should have been discovered in volunteers before marketing.

Opren showed, once again the need to concentrate on the right species — man.

R.S.

Source: *Bulletin 19, The Lord Dowding Fund*

4 HOW TO GET ADDRESSES

Often you will want to write off for information but will not know what specialist organisations exist. You may know of an organisation and want to know the address. Some school libraries have lists of useful addresses on file cards or on computer. Alternatively many reference libraries contain telephone directories for the whole country and also a large number of specialist directories. Particularly useful for obtaining addresses is *Whitaker's Almanac*. This is a book which is published every year. As well as containing a wide range of useful facts such as major events taking place during the year, employment statistics etc., there is also a list of addresses of all major societies and basic details about the work of all government and public offices. Another useful source of addresses may be *Voluntary Organisations: an N.C.V.O. Directory 1985/6*, published by Bedford Square Press/National Council for Voluntary Organisations. This lists 800 voluntary organisations with brief details on activities and publications plus all the relevant current addresses.

Often, if you cannot find an address or want to know if there is a local branch of an organisation which you can contact, it is worth telephoning your local Information Office to see if they can help you.

CRIMINAL INJURIES COMPENSATION BOARD
Whittington House, 19 Alfred Place, WC1E 7LG
[01–636 9501 and 01–631 4467]

The Board was constituted in 1964 to administer the Government scheme for *ex gratia* payments of compensation to victims of crimes of violence.
Chairman, M. Ogden, Q.C.;
Members, I. J. Black, Q.C.; M. S. R. Bruce, Q.C.; D. Calcutt, Q.C.; H. Carlisle, Q.C.; B. W. Chedlow, Q.C.; Miss B. Cooper, Q.C.; J. D. Crowley, Q.C.; Sir Richard Denby; C. Fawcett, Q.C.; Sir Arthur Hoole; J. Law, Q.C.; Sir Denis Marshall; M. Morland, Q.C.; The Lord Morton of Shuna, Q.C.; A. S. Myerson, Q.C.; C. W. F. Newman, Q.C.; Sir John Palmer; I. M. S. Park, C.B.E.; F. H. Potts, Q.C.; Miss S. Ritchie, Q.C.; D. B. Robertson, Q.C.; L. Stuart Shields, Q.C.; D. M. Thomas, O.B.E.; Q.C.; C. H. Whitby, Q.C.
Secretary and Solicitor, D. M. North.
Deputy Secretary, D. J. White.
Chief Executive, T. F. Corbett.

NATIONAL SOCIETY FOR THE PREVENTION OF CRUELTY TO CHILDREN (1884), *Headquarters*, 67 Saffron Hill EC1N 8RS—*Chairman*, Lady Holland-Martin, D.B.E., D.L.; *Hon. Treas.*, M. Weinberg; *Dir.*, Dr. A. Gilmour, C.B.E.
NATIONAL UNION OF STUDENTS, 461 Holloway Road N7 6LJ—*Nat. Sec.*, J. Doran.
NATIONAL VIEWERS' AND LISTENERS' ASSOCIATION.— *President*, Mrs. M. Whitehouse, C.B.E, Blachernae, Ardleigh, Colchester, Essex CO7 7RH.
NATION'S FUND FOR NURSES, 57 Lower Belgrave Street SW1W 0LR—*Administrator*, P. E. Starr.
NATURE CONSERVATION, ROYAL SOCIETY FOR (1912).— *Gen. Sec.*, Dr. F. H. Perring, The Green, Nettleham, Lincoln LN2 2NR.

DEVELOPMENT COMMISSION
11 Cowley Street, SW1P 3NA
[01-222 9134]

The Development Commission, England's rural development agency, is a statutory body funded by Government grant-in-aid which undertakes economic and social problems in rural areas and advises the Government on related rural matters in England. It concentrates its resources in priority areas—Rural Development Areas—but some assistance, particularly through its main agency, the Council for Small

Extracts from Whitaker's Almanac

CHECKLIST

- Make sure that your address for reply is clearly included.

- Be clear about what exactly you want to say before writing — what exactly do you want to know from this person?

- Start by explaining who you are and what exactly you are interested in.

- Make sure that your questions are clear and that you don't ask too many.

- Type or write clearly.

- Include a stamped addressed envelope for reply. This is particularly important when writing to pressure groups which are charitable organisations and do not have vast funds.

- Write in plenty of time; organisations often take a few weeks to reply so allow for this. If you have a deadline for reply say so. If you need a really quick reply it might be better to telephone rather than write.

- Get someone to check your letter before you post it.

- Keep a copy of your letter.

- When you receive a reply to your letter, pick out any important points and discuss them in your project; do not just put in the reply.

Chapter Six
Using Libraries

For most topics of research there is already a lot of information available which you can use. This includes:

- newspaper reports
- statistics collected by the government and other people
- research which other people have done into your subject
- leaflets produced by interested groups
- historical documents

Before you begin your own project it is important to look at some of this information to see how you can use it.

1 WHERE TO FIND INFORMATION

For many projects the information that you need will be available in your school library or in your local lending library. It may also be obtainable by writing to different organisations as explained earlier. There are, however, two central sources of information which you may find helpful.

CHAPTER 5

1.1 The County Record Office

Most counties in Britain have a Central Record Office. The Record Office keeps a huge variety of materials on local history. This can be used, for example, to look at the way a village or town has developed, to look at changes in crime and punishment, changes in housing or to trace a family tree. The actual materials kept vary, but there are usually local census returns (except for the last one hundred years), a collection of maps, records of the local courts, parish records and County and District Council records. Many of these records are stored on microfiche to save space. You'll need to ask the librarian to help you obtain this information. All Record Offices have staff who will help you to find the information which you need although it is advisable to telephone or write first to let them know what you are interested in. It is also important that you have a fairly clear idea of what you want to find out. If you use the Record Office you must be prepared to spend a fair amount of time sorting through documents to find the information which is relevant to your topic.

1.2 The Central Reference Library

Almost all towns have a Central Reference Library or Information Centre. Although this is part of the Libraries and Information Service it is often separate from the Central Lending Library. The exact information contained in a reference library varies from town to town. When you have a clear idea of what you want to find out it is worth telephoning or writing to see if they have what you need. There are qualified staff who can help you and although books normally cannot be taken away there is usually a photocopying service. The main types of information which you may find useful are statistical records, newspapers and magazines, directories, address books and other reference books.

2 COMPUTER DATABASES

An increasing amount of information is stored on computer databases. This is usually statistical information and may include local and national census figures, and other statistics based on surveys of the population. An example of computer software which could be useful for social science research is the series published by Longmans on women, class and poverty. These computer tapes contain a vast amount of statistics based on the general household survey of 1979. New computer software is being developed all the time and it is worth asking your library what is available. As well as published computer software it may be possible to get information on, for example, subject option choices from the school computer.

3 PROBLEMS IN USING PRINTED MATERIAL

If you use any published information you must find out as much as you can about the source of the information. You must be aware that all information could be biased (one-sided). This can be true as much of statistics as of newspapers. For all sources you must ask:

- Who produced the information and why?
- Do they support a particular cause?
- Are there likely to be any things missed out?
- Is the information given in a way which supports one point of view rather than another?

For other people's research you should ask:

- How good was the sample?
- Is everyone included or are certain people missed out?
- How clear were the questions?

When you write up information which you get from books, magazines, leaflets or other printed material explain how you think it might be biased. For any printed information you use, always note down the exact reference — title, author, page, date and any other relevant points.

ACTIVITY

The next three chapters discuss ways in which you can use materials from libraries. Choose one of the following topics, or a topic of your own. Visit your local reference library and list all the different kinds of information you can find on your topic. Your list could include statistics, newspaper reports, addresses and other studies or articles.

Possible topics:

- Child abuse
- Drugs
- Football hooliganism
- A recent news event, e.g. a strike or a demonstration
- Cot deaths
- Unemployment
- A local issue, e.g. plans for housing development or building a by-pass.

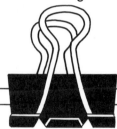

CHECKLIST

- Have a fairly clear idea of what you want to find out before visiting a library.

- If you need particular information sources such as old newspapers or census figures it is worth telephoning beforehand to check that the library keeps them.

- Find out any special rules the library may have before you go: for example, Record Offices usually only allow you to take notes in pencil.

- Always keep a full record of any references which you use; this should include the title, author, page reference and date of publication.

- Read printed information critically. Always think about whether anything has been missed out or if there is any bias. This is particularly important with newspaper reports.

Chapter Seven
Using Statistics

Statistics are just lists of numbers which show how many people fit into certain categories. These are often based on the census or on social surveys. You can use statistics in your project as background information or to actually answer your research questions. The examples in this chapter have been chosen to show you both where you can get statistics from, and how you can use them.

Statistical tables are often difficult to understand. You may, at first, need someone to explain how they have been set out. Some of the things that you should look for in reading statistics are shown in the table below which shows the percentage of males and females in each social class (socio-economic group) who smoked in different years.

Notice how the figures are described. Here it is percentages. Sometimes, the number of people will be expressed in thousands. In such cases, you must remember to add three noughts on to every figure ↓

Always read the title, it explains exactly what the table shows →

Adult[1] cigarette smoking: by sex and socio-economic group[2]

Great Britain — *Percentages and numbers*

	Socio-economic group							Average cigarette con-sumption per smoker
	Pro-fessional	Employers and managers	Inter-mediate and junior non-manual	Skilled manual and own account non-pro-fessional	Semi-skilled manual and personal service	Un-skilled manual	All persons[3]	
Percentage smoking cigarettes								
Males								
1972	33	44	45	57	57	64	52	120
1976	25	38	40	51	53	58	46	129
1980	21	35	35	48	49	57	42	124
1982	20	29	30	42	47	49	38	121
1984	17	29	30	40	45	49	36	115
1984 Sample size (numbers)	448	1,413	1,384	3,063	1,350	478	8,417	
Females								
1972	33	38	38	47	42	42	42	87
1976	28	35	36	42	41	38	38	101
1980	21	33	34	43	39	41	37	102
1982	21	29	30	39	36	41	33	98
1984	15	29	28	37	37	36	32	96
1984 Sample size (numbers)	384	1,487	2,436	2,585	1,864	518	9,788	

If you read down the columns you can see how the percentage of smokers has changed over time →

This entry tells you the number of people who were included in the study →

[1] Persons aged 15 or over in 1972, but 16 or over in later years.
[2] See Appendix, Part 7: General Household Survey.

[3] Includes members of the armed forces, people in inadequately described occupations, and all people who have never worked.
Source: General Household Survey

Source: Social Trends 16, HMSO 1986, p.113

Always look at the notes: they will help you to understand the table. Here Note 1 tells you that in 1972 the term 'adults' referred to people over 15; in other years it referred to people over 16. This is useful to know if you want to repeat the research yourself

If you read across the table, you can see — for any one year — the difference in the percentage of people smoking in each social class

1 WHERE TO FIND STATISTICS AND HOW TO USE THEM

Statistics may often be found in text books or obtained by writing off to organisations. If, however, you want more specialist or more detailed statistics there are three main sources which you could use.

1.1 Social Trends

Social Trends is a book published by H.M.S.O. every year. It summarises statistics which have been collected on the population of Britain. It is divided into twelve sections: population; households and families; education; employment; income and wealth; resources and expenditure; health and personal social services; housing; transport; communication and the environment; leisure; participation and law employment.

Most statistics are presented in a way which allows you to see how things have changed over time.

ACTIVITY

Using the table on page 48 on smoking, reproduced from *Social Trends*, answer the following questions:

1 Using the column labelled 'All persons':
   (a) In what way did the percentage of males who smoked change between 1972 and 1984?
   (b) In what way did the percentage of females who smoked change between 1972 and 1984?
   (c) In 1984 who was more likely to smoke, males or females?

2 Using 1984 only, reading across:
   (a) In what social class are males most likely to smoke?
   (b) In what social class are females most likely to smoke?

Using this table you could draw up graphs to show, for example, the percentage of males who smoke compared with females or the percentage of people who smoke in each social class.

CHAPTER 2

CHAPTER 3

You could then go on to give out a questionnaire to find out teenage attitudes towards smoking and could say whether you think the fall in the number of people who smoke will continue. Alternatively you could interview people or give out a questionnaire to try to find out the reasons why fewer people smoke now than in the past.

Social Trends is often kept in school libraries or in local lending libraries for reference only. Failing this it will almost certainly be found in the Central Reference Library. If you need more detailed statistics reference libraries have many sources. The most useful are those based on the population census and those based on the registrations of births, marriages and deaths. There are also detailed statistics on such things as family spending patterns (*The Family Expenditure Survey*) and the workings of the social security system (published by H.M.S.O./D.H.S.S.).

1.2 The Population Census

The Census is carried out every ten years. It is information based on a questionnaire completed by every household in Britain. A census is more than just a head count; it gives a lot of information about the British population.

The actual questions vary a little between censuses but the main topics for the 1981 census were:

- basic population information (age, sex, marital status)
- migration (address one year before 1981 to measure movement within the country)
- country of birth
- economic activity (employment/unemployment, type of job)
- education and professional qualifications
- composition of families and households (e.g. family size)
- accommodation (privately owned/rented etc.), number of rooms and amenities such as toilet/bath etc.)

The census is delivered to all households by a trained person known as an enumerator. He or she then collects the completed forms.

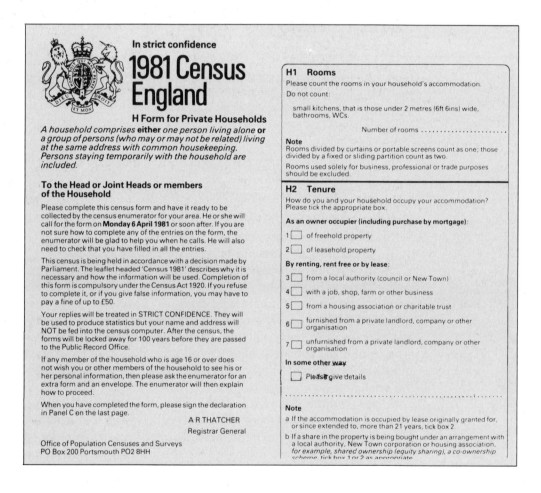

The information gained from a census is produced in statistical tables which are usually available in reference libraries. It is possible to look at census information for different areas of the country or for the population as a whole.

Although large numbers of women work outside the home, many are still employed in 'women's' jobs, such as domestic work or packing. Very few women are employed in traditionally male roles

ACTIVITY

The table below shows the number of married women in Britain who worked outside the home in 1981 depending on the age of their children. The figures are for Great Britain as a whole; in the census booklet the figures are also given for every area within Great Britain so that you could compare, for example, north and south.

Economic position of married women

GREAT BRITAIN

| | | In households with: | |
Economic position	No children under 16	Child(ren) aged 0–4 with or without child(ren) aged 5–15	Child(ren) aged 5–15 only
a	b	c	d
All married women	6,950,357	2,187,484	3,424,686
Economically active	3,246,799	547,628	2,114,560
In employment	3,126,377	487,372	2,050,041
working full-time	1,870,275	128,890	699,545
working part-time	1,256,102	358,482	1,350,496
Economically inactive	3,703,558	1,639,856	1,310,126

Source: National Report, *1981 Census, page 216*

Below are some questions on this information:

1 How many married women were there in Britain in 1981? (add up 'All married women' in the three columns across the page)
2 How many married women were 'In employment' in 1981?
3 How does having children affect the work of married women? Can you explain why women with no children under the age of sixteen are less likely to work outside the home than women with children between the ages of five and sixteen? Think about the ages of the women.
4 Can you think of any research questions which you could now go on to look at related to this topic? What methods of investigation could you use?

One advantage of a census is the fact that it is filled in by the whole population and is therefore as accurate as it is possible for statistics to be. One difficulty is that some of the statistics are quite complicated and you may need help sorting through them.

1.3 Registration of births, marriages and deaths

All births, marriages and deaths in Great Britain must be registered with the Registrar General. From this the Office of Population Censuses and Surveys produce a number of volumes of detailed statistics each year. Birth statistics show, for example, the number of legitimate and illegitimate births each year, the social class of parents, the ages of both parents, the number of still births and the average family size. Any of these facts can also be seen with others giving, for example, the number of still births in each social class. Marriage and divorce statistics can give information on the number of marriages and remarriages, the number of divorces, the age (at marriage) of people who get divorced, the number and age of children in divorcing families etc. Mortality (death) statistics give, for example, information on the causes of death at different ages and in different classes.

All of these statistics are fairly complicated but they do provide detailed information. The diagrams below and on the next page give information on the number of legitimate and illegitimate births between 1974 and 1984.

Percentage of live births which were illegitimate 1974 to 1984

ACTIVITY

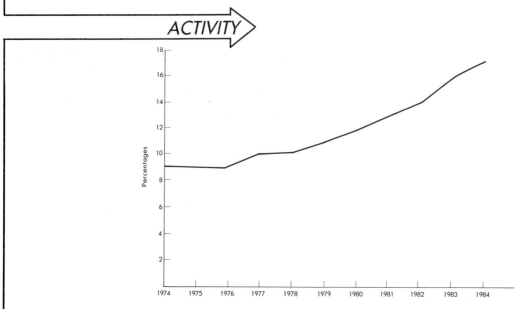

Source: Based on Birth Statistics: 1984, the office of Population Censuses and Surveys, p.31

Pie charts to show the percentage of births which were legitimate and illegitimate for mothers of different ages, 1984

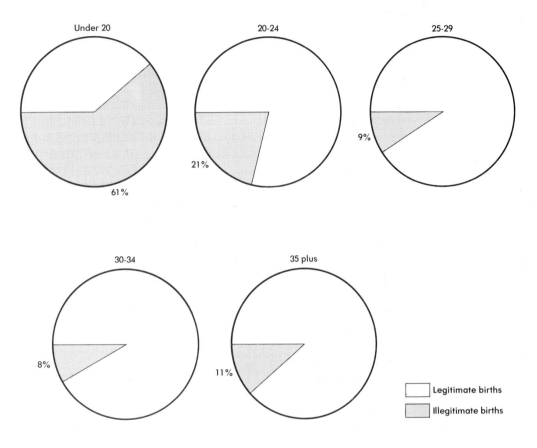

Source: *Adapted from* Birth Statistics: *1984*, the Office of Population Censuses and Surveys, p.31

Below are some questions on these diagrams:
- By how much has the percentage of live illegitimate births changed in the ten year period shown in the graph? Can you suggest any explanations for this increase?
- How does the percentage of illegitimate live births vary with the mother's age? What explanations can you offer for this?
- Can you think of any research questions which you could now go on to look at on this topic?

2. How accurate are statistics?

In all of the examples given in this chapter statistics have been used as background research or to give factual information to answer a question. Statistics can also be used in a more critical way.

Statistics are not always completely accurate, some cases may be left out or they may be biased. Whereas all births in Britain are likely to be recorded, many crimes or cases of, for example, drug abuse or illness, go unrecorded. Whether a crime enters the statistics depends on whether it is reported to the police or observed by them. Many crimes are not reported by victims or witnesses (see article on page 58) and the police observe only a small proportion of all crimes. Some areas of your town may appear to have a low crime rate, not because there is no crime but because there are very few policemen patrolling the area. Even when a crime has been reported or observed it may not enter the statistics, the police may decide not to prosecute. We say that crime statistics are **SOCIALLY CONSTRUCTED**; this means that rather than including all crimes they depend on decisions that have been made about which areas to patrol and about who to prosecute. The activity on page 57 in Chapter 8 is designed to help you understand the problems with these figures. It may be worth completing this activity before going on.

ACTIVITY

Which of the following types of statistics are 'socially constructed'? In each case, explain how these statistics might be biased; what people might be included or left out, who makes the decisions. Discuss your answers.

- Registered drug addicts
- Death rates
- Child abuse
- Number of people suffering from mental illness
- Infant mortality rates in Britain
- Cot deaths
- Poverty

CHECKLIST

- Always explain what tables mean and how they fit into your project. You should never include tables which you do not understand.

- Always say from where you got your statistics and, if possible, how accurate or complete you think they are. For example, crime statistics only tell us about crimes which have been reported.

- Try to present statistical information in a variety of attractive ways including graphs, charts or pictograms.

Chapter Eight
Using Published Research

Large amounts of research are done every year, not just by government bodies but by market research organisations and by sociologists. Reports of research can be found in books, although these may be both very difficult and very detailed. Other sources of research information include newspapers and magazines such as *New Society*. Sometimes useful research may be summarised in sociology text books; your teacher may be able to help you find these. *New Society* has a 'findings' section which summarises briefly any new findings. Most magazines have their own yearly index which is arranged by topic as well as by author and title of the article. There are also other useful indexes which may be kept by local reference libraries. One of these is the *CLOVER Information Index* which is published several times a year and put together into a single volume at the end of the year. This classifies articles from a large number of magazines. It is arranged in topic order, alphabetically, so it is possible to look up your topic and find a list of articles which have been written during the year which may be useful to you. The following extract from the *CLOVER Information Index* lists articles on 'Women' in 1985.

WOMEN: HISTORY
  What is women's history? HT 6.85 p34–48
WOMEN: SCIENCE: HISTORY
  Pen is mightier than the test-tube NS
  14.2.85 p56–8
WOMEN: USA: HISTORY
  Feminism and Republicanism, American
  motherhood HT 12.84 p28–33
WOMEN: WINE
  Women and wine WMK 8.85 p18–20
WOMEN: WORKING MOTHERS
  Two worlds GH 5.85 p.141 – Special
  section
WOMEN'S REFUGES
  Fall-out in the refuges NSO 28.6.85
  p488–9

Source: CLOVER Information Index 1985, p293–4.
NSO = *New Society*
NI = *New Internationalist*
HT = *History Today*
WMK = *Wine Maker*
GH = *Good Housekeeping*

You can look up references in a large number of magazines by using the *British Humanities Index*, available in many reference libraries. This is arranged alphabetically by subject, but is fairly difficult to understand because many topics are cross-referenced and you may need to ask the librarian for help.

Many useful magazines such as *New Society* and the *New Internationalist* may be kept in your school library but, failing that, should be in the Central Reference Library. As for statistics much of this information will be fairly difficult to understand and you must decide how important it is in your research. There are several ways in which you can use published research in your project.

1 USING PUBLISHED RESEARCH FOR BACKGROUND INFORMATION

When planning your project it is useful to use other people's research to get ideas and to help you sort out your main questions or hypothesis. When using other people's research you will be interested in the results rather than the methods used. If you use research in this way you should describe briefly how it has helped you but do not need to discuss the findings or research methods in great detail.

2 TESTING OR REPEATING PUBLISHED RESEARCH

You may wish to use research for more than background reading. You could actually test the findings of research by repeating it yourself. For example research by Ann Oakley (*The Sociology of Housework*, Basil Blackwell, 1974) showed that in the 1970s most families did not share their roles, that is, to a large extent women still took the main responsibility for childcare and housework. You could repeat this research perhaps to find out whether families are different in the 1980s or to find out whether role sharing is different when women work outside the home.

In the 1970s William Belson carried out a survey to find out the attitudes which the general public had towards the police. (*The Public and the Police*, Harper and Row, 1975). He asked 1200 adults, 503 teenagers and 1000 policemen to fill in a questionnaire to find general attitudes of young people and adults to the police. He was also interested in where people got their ideas about the police from — was it from direct experience or from the media or from gossip? He found that the public were generally satisfied but that they did have some criticisms of police methods. He also found that most people had very little knowledge of police work and that negative opinions were usually based not on direct experience but information from newspapers, television or gossip. You could repeat this research to find out if attitudes have changed as a result of the riots and disturbances of recent years.

Large amounts of research have been done to discover whether boys and girls are treated differently in schools. This research could be repeated in your own school to find out, for example, to what extent equal opportunities exist.

In all of these cases you could use the same methods as the original research. For example, you could repeat Belson's questionnaire, or you could prepare your own. If you are using published research in this way you must:

- Describe the research quite fully, the methods and the findings,
- discuss any problems with the research (e.g. a poor sample or biased questions),
- explain exactly what you want to test and why,
- describe your own methods of research,
- write up your results and comments on them and
- compare your results with those of the earlier study. How do they differ? Why do you think this is?

3 USING PUBLISHED RESEARCH TO TEST YOUR HYPOTHESIS OR TO ANSWER YOUR QUESTIONS

If you do not have enough time to carry out your own research, or if the information you need is too difficult for you to get by yourself, you could use published research to test your own hypothesis. For example official crime statistics show that crime is going up rapidly and that the 'typical' criminal is a male, working class teenager. You could carry out a piece of research to find out if this picture of crime is actually correct.

ACTIVITY

Below are two extracts from published research. How could you use this information in your project to test the accuracy of crime statistics?

Offences admitted by a sample of young persons in Utah, USA, and per cent undetected and unacted upon.

Offence	Per cent admitting	Offences admitted	Unde-tected	Unacted upon
Theft				
Articles less than $2	93	15,175	97·1	99·8
Articles worth $2 to $50	59	7,396	97·1	99·1
Articles more than $50	26	294	71·0	92·8
Car theft	29	822	88·9	95·5
Forgery	13	512	93·4	97·5
Total		24,199	96·3	99·3
Offences against person				
Armed robbery	5	46	80·4	91·3
Fighting, assault	70	8,980	99·7	99·9
Total	—	9,026	99·6	99·9
Property violations				
Breaking and entering	59	1,622	85·6	94·4
Destroying property	80	10,645	98·5	99·7
Starting fires (arson)	6	11	40·0	90·0
Total	—	12,278	96·8	99·0

Source: Adapted from Hood and Sparkes, Key Issues in Criminology, *World University Press, 1972, p.24*

This table summarises some of the findings of a **SELF REPORT STUDY** in America. In this type of study people are asked to admit to any crimes which they have committed including any which have not been detected (found out about) or acted upon by the police.

The Hidden Crime Wave

EXCLUSIVE
by Martin Kettle

MANY more crimes are committed in Britain than official figures disclose, according to a government report due to be published next month.

For every theft reported to the police, four go unreported. For crimes of violence, five victims do not bother to tell the police for every one who does.

These startling figures emerge from the first national victim-based survey carried out by the Home Office. It shows that in most cases, the victims did not consider the crimes serious enough to justify telling the police.

The survey covered 11,000 households in England and Wales and was carried out in February and March 1982. A similar survey of 6,000 Scottish households took place at the same time. All the householders were asked how often in the past year they had been the victims of crime, and whether or not they informed the police.

Under-reporting, the survey shows, differs dramatically between different types of crime. Most car thefts are reported because of insurance claims and the need for police help in getting the car back. But there are twice as many unreported burglaries and 13 times as many acts of vandalism as those in the official statistics.

Home Office ministers are worried that publication of the report will provoke sensationalised public fears that crime has suddenly gone out of control, even though the survey suggests that the average Briton's chance of being the victim of a serious crime is remarkably low.

The average household can expect to be burgled once every 40 years. Although the risk of burglary is greater in inner city areas, it is correspondingly lower in the country.

Previous victim studies of burglary have shown that commonly imagined rises in crime are less dramatic than supposed. One commonly accepted belief that the new survey is likely to dispel is that the elderly, far from being the group most likely to be the victim of violent crime, are in fact the least at risk.

Home Office ministers believe that the survey provides no justification for massive new increases in police manpower or in powers for the courts. Instead, they are reacting by pressing the police to redeploy their large existing resources into joint crime prevention efforts with local communities.

The home secretary, William Whitelaw, is already giving enthusiastic backing to this strategy in London, where it is being introduced by the new head of Scotland Yard, Sir Kenneth Newman. Last week, Whitelaw launched an anti-burglary campaign which is seen as a key element in the process.

Source: The Sunday Times, *13th February 1983*

4 USING PUBLISHED RESEARCH: AN EXAMPLE

In 1986 *New Society* magazine carried out a survey to find out what teenagers in England and Wales felt on a number of issues (see extract on the next page). They contacted social science teachers throughout the country and asked them to give out questionnaires in their lessons. The questionnaires were to be filled in privately and placed in a sealed envelope before they were returned to the teacher. More than five hundred schools and colleges took part and 15,000 questionnaires were completed. The researchers then reduced this to a random sample of 2417. This was arranged so that different regions of England and Wales were represented. There were twice as many girls as boys, 82 per cent of the sample were white, five per cent Asian, five per cent black and two per cent other races. Most of the students were studying for exams — CSE, O-level or A-level. Clearly the type of people included in the sample is influenced by the sort of students who choose to study social science subjects; this explains why there were more girls than boys, for example. The survey was analysed by the market research organisation Gallup, to produce a large number of tables. The results were summarised in *New Society* on 21 February 1986 and an extract from the questionnaire and a summary of the findings appears on the following page.

ATSS/NEW SOCIETY SURVEY (extract)

Question One

School ....

Age ....

Sex ....
What subject are you studying in this class?

....

What exam are you working for?
Please tick

CSE	☐1
GCSE	☐2
O level	☐3
A level	☐4
Vocational qualification (please specify)	
....	☐5
Other (please specify)	
....	☐6
None	☐7

Question Two
How likely is it, do you think, that you will get a job when you have finished your studies? Please tick.

(a)	Very likely	☐1
(b)	Quite likely	☐2
(c)	Not very likely	☐3
(d)	A very small chance	☐4
(e)	Totally unlikely	☐5
(f)	I have a job already	☐6

Question Three
Which of these reasons do you think most accounts for the high level of joblessness in society? You may tick more than one.

(a)	The government has the wrong policies	☐1
(b)	New technology means that unemployment is inevitable	☐2
(c)	The unions have priced people out of jobs	☐3
(d)	Industry has been hit by events outside Britain's control	☐4
(e)	It is too easy to exist on social security	☐5
(f)	The unemployed are basically lazy and don't want jobs	☐6

Question Four
How satisfied are you with the education you are getting at your school or college? Please tick.

(a)	Highly satisfied	☐1
(b)	Satisfied	☐2
(c)	Fairly satisfied	☐3
(d)	Not satisfied	☐4
(e)	Totally dissatisfied	☐5

Question Five
Please state briefly how you think it could be improved. (You may use an extra sheet of paper if you need to.)

....
....
....
....
....
....

Question Six
How would you rate yourself in your political views? Please tick the one that comes closest to how you see yourself.

(a)	Left-wing	☐1
(b)	Centrist	☐2
(c)	Right-wing	☐3
(d)	Inclined towards ecological issues	☐4
(e)	Not political	☐5

Question Seven
How do you think that you compare with your parents' generation in terms of the general opportunities that you have in your life? Please tick.

(a)	Very much better off than your parents	☐1
(b)	Better off than your parents	☐2
(c)	About the same	☐3
(d)	Worse off	☐4
(e)	Very much worse off	☐5

Question Eight
Some people say that British governments nowadays — of whichever party — can actually do little to change things. Others suggest they can do quite a bit. Which of these statements do you most agree with? Please tick.

(a)	Governments can change things if they want to	☐1
(b)	Governments are fairly powerless to change things	☐2

School and jobs

Most of the students were either satisfied or fairly satisfied with the education they were receiving and surprisingly most felt that they would get a job on leaving school. Over three-quarters either already had a job or felt that they were quite likely to get one. When asked to suggest reasons for unemployment a very small percentage of all ages thought that the unemployed were lazy, that it was easy to live on social security or that the unions were responsible. The commonest answers to this question blamed government policies or new technology.

Politics

Nearly half (40%) of the students said that they were not political. As would be expected, the younger age groups gave this answer more than the older age groups (54% of under-14s compared with 23% of over-19s). Of those who gave a political view most claimed to be left wing (22%) or centrist (21%).

Drugs

The results of the two questions asked on drugs are shown in the table.

	total	male	female	under-14	14—16	over-19	north of England	south of Engand	Wales	Asian	West Indian	white	other
Total in sample	2,417	725	1,692	235	977	213	1,140	1,145	133	128	132	1,974	47
Which of the following drugs have you tried? (Figures given are percentages.)													
cigarettes	65	64	65	60	67	69	63	66	65	37	60	67	61
cannabis	17	24	14	7	12	37	14	19	25	7	15	18	18
heroin	2	3	1	3	1	5	2	2	1	0	4	2	6
solvents	6	10	4	8	6	6	5	7	2	5	2	6	4
alcohol	89	90	88	85	88	82	90	87	88	54	76	92	88
not stated	7	6	8	10	8	10	6	8	9	33	16	5	8
Which of the following drugs do you think is most dangerous in terms of the effect it has on society in general? (Figures given are percentages.)													
cigarettes	21	22	20	14	20	25	21	20	21	20	18	21	14
cannabis	2	2	1	3	1	1	2	2	0	2	1	1	2
heroin	56	55	57	71	61	40	56	57	56	57	66	56	61
solvents	5	4	5	3	5	3	5	5	6	7	4	5	6
alcohol	16	16	16	8	12	29	16	15	16	12	11	17	13
not stated	1	1	1	1	1	2	1	1	0	1	1	1	4

Source: New Society, *21st February 1986, pp312/313.*

Attitudes on sexual behaviour

Students were asked questions on their attitudes towards contraception being available for girls under sixteen without their parents' consent and towards pre-marital, extra-marital (outside marriage) and homosexual relationships. Generally there was little support for the ideas of immoral or permissive behaviour by teenagers which is often suggested by the mass media. Most felt that doctors should tell parents in exceptional circumstances if they were prescribing contraceptives for girls under sixteen; only 16% felt that parents should never be told. There was fairly general agreement that pre-marital sexual relationships were acceptable; only 4% thought that this was always wrong and 59% thought that it was not wrong at all.

In contrast most students felt that extra-marital sexual relationships were wrong. There was a slight tendency here for males to feel that these relationships were more acceptable than females. Attitudes towards homosexuality were fairly divided with 32% feeling that it was always wrong and 29% believing that it was not wrong at all. Generally females and older people were more tolerant than males and younger people.

Attitudes towards sex equality

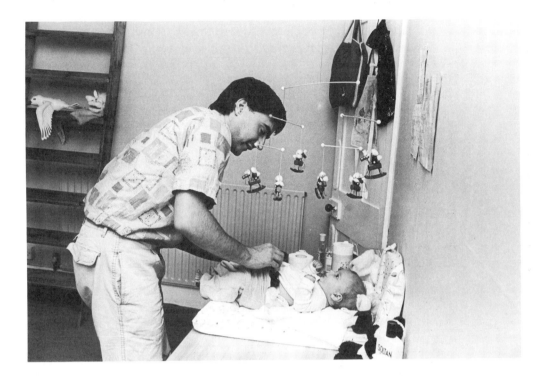

On sex equality females argued very strongly that most roles should be shared equally whereas males had a slightly more traditional view of who should do what in the home. The table shows the percentage of males and females who felt that each role should be shared equally.

	Males (%)	Females (%)
Washing and ironing	48	62
Preparation of evening meal	62	80
Household cleaning	59	80
Household shopping	71	83
Choice of living room colour	82	90
Washing-up	75	88
Organisation of household money and bills	65	80
Repairs of household equipment	36	52

Source: adapted from New Society/ATSS *Survey, unpublished results*

Generally Asians were slightly less in favour of sharing roles equally than the sample as a whole whereas West Indians were more strongly in favour of equality.

Racial attitudes

One of the most depressing findings came in reply to the questions of racial prejudice. Altogether 42% of whites said that they were prejudiced to some extent against people of other races. West Indians were as strongly prejudiced as whites, whereas three-quarters of Asians said that they were not prejudiced at all.

Beliefs

The students were asked how much they believed in such things as ghosts and flying saucers. The table below shows the percentage of students who said that they believed either quite a lot or some of the time.

	Males (%)	Females (%)
Ghosts	56	61
Life after death	57	70
The existence of God	61	73
Horoscopes	37	59
Tarot cards	29	35
Lucky charms or mascots	39	44
Flying saucers	57	30
Thought transference between two people	62	63
Faith healing	52	57

Source: Adapted from New Society/ATSS Survey, *unpublished results*

Where did the young people get their information from?

The percentage claiming to get information from different sources is shown in the graph.

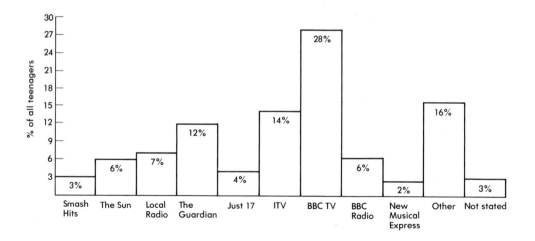

Source: Adapted from New Society/ATSS Survey, *unpublished results, 1986*

ACTIVITY

Read the report and findings carefully and answer the following questions:
1 What was the study trying to find out?
2 Re-read the section on problems in using printed material on page 46. Do you think that there are any problems with this study? Think particularly about how they got their sample and any ways in which this may be biased (likely to include certain types of people rather than others). Look also at the questions and the way in which they are worded; how easy would you find them to answer?
3 There are a large number of findings you could use for a basis of your own research. Pick out two findings and say how you could use them in your research — what research questions could you ask and how could you go about the research?

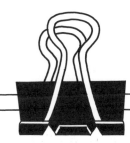

CHECKLIST

- Use indexes, textbooks and magazines to find out if any research has been done on your topic. In your project, describe how you found this research.

- Note down when the research was done, what methods were used and what the results were.

- Decide how you intend to use this research in your project — as background, to repeat the research yourself, or to test your hypothesis. Follow the guidelines on using research in the different sections of this chapter.

- Always try to say how good a piece of research was in terms of its methods.

Chapter Nine
Using Newspapers

For events which have happened fairly recently newspapers may be a major source of information. Most reference libraries keep a number of national newspapers such as *The Times, The Guardian* or *The Mirror* as well as local daily papers. In most libraries at least one paper (usually *The Times*) is likely to be kept for many years although most papers will be destroyed after a few months due to lack of storage space. There are two main ways in which you can use newspapers in your project. You can use them to find out background information on a topic or event, or you can study newspapers in more detail looking at the way in which they report particular events. When using newspapers you must always try to find out if the paper is biased in any way.

1 USING NEWSPAPERS FOR INFORMATION

Newspapers will provide very useful information on topics such as drug offences, football hooliganism and cases of child abuse. Often with events such as strikes or political meetings, this information can only be obtained from newspapers. Usually it is enough to collect newspaper articles which appear while you are writing your project although sometimes you may want to find past articles. An example would be the miners' strike in 1984/1985.

It is possible to find reports on any subject in *The Times* by using *The Times Index*. This is published annually and lists all articles on a wide range of topics which have appeared in any *Times* newspaper during the year. The subjects are arranged alphabetically and the index gives the date, page and column, plus the title or a brief summary.

EXAMPLE: CHILD ABUSE PROJECT
If a project was on child abuse you would look up 'Children and young people'. Under this is the sub-heading 'Cruelty and neglect' and a long list of relevant articles. A small section of this reference in the 1985 *Index* is shown below.

Articles—"The unacceptable fate of British childhood", (ST) SEPT. 22, 4a; "The cruel facts of child abuse in Britain", 26, 12a; "Panic is not a solution", (ST) 29, 16b; 'Can common sense halt child abuse?", (ST) DEC. 8, 18a; "A child in care, a child in trust", (TES) 13, 4a
Babies born to drug addicts: see DRUG addiction, abuse and traffic: Babies born to addicts
Beckford (Jasmin) case: see MURDER, manslaughter and related charges: Beckford, Jasmin
Correspondence, APR. 3, 15d; MAY 9, 15f; SEPT. 21, 9d; 26, 15d; 27, 13d; OCT. 1, 17e; (ST) 6, 26a; Nov. 30, 9e; DEC. 6, 17d; 7, 9f; 10, 11d; 13, 11d; (ST) 15, 9b; 18, 11d

Girl starved to death: see MURDER, manslaughter and related charges: Koseda, Heidi
Hartwell (Gemma) case: see MURDER, manslaughter and related charges: Hartwell, Gemma
Henry (Tyra) case: see MURDER, manslaughter and related charges: Henry, Tyra
Leading article, APR. 12, 15a; 18, 17a, JULY 27, 9a; DEC. 4, 15a
Parliament discussed, MAY 1, 4a; JULY 27, 4d; Nov. 30, 2d; DEC. 4, 4d
Salt (Charlene) case: see MURDER, manslaughter and related charges: Salt, Charlene

Source: The Times Index, *1985, p.169*

These are all articles which appeared in 1985. You could look up the same topic for any other year. If you want to look up a particular case of child abuse you can find all of the newspaper reports so long as you know the year in which it happened. Using newspapers other than *The Times* is more difficult because there is not an index and you would have to sort through each individual copy to find what you wanted. Unless you knew the date of each article that you were looking for, this would be very difficult. Sometimes you can get newspaper cuttings by writing to the newspapers and asking for photocopies; this may, however, be expensive. Some reference libraries also keep cuttings files on subjects in which they think people might be interested.

2 ANALYSING NEWSPAPERS

You may need to study newspapers more closely, not just to get information from them but to see how they treat a particular group of people or a particular event. For example you could study the way newspapers report young people or women or unemployment. Alternatively you could look at how different newspapers report the same event such as a strike. When analysing newspapers there are several things you should look at.

Headlines

Most people read the headlines first before deciding whether to read an article. Some people just read the paper quickly and may *only* read the headlines. Headlines, therefore, need to stand out and to capture the reader's attention. They need to be quite simple but must also sum up the article. The two headlines below appeared in two national daily papers on the same day, reporting the same event. The event was the health workers' 'day of action' in 1982. Notice that they give a very different opinion of what actually happened.

THE GREAT PROTEST
(*The Mirror*)

THE DAY THAT CHANGED NOTHING
(*The Daily Mail*)

Photographs

Photographs, like headlines, need to attract the readers' attention. As with headlines they are also useful in telling the reader what to think about the issue. Most photographs have a caption underneath which tells you how to read the photograph; often the same photograph with a different caption can give a different message. The photograph on the right appeared in the front page of several national dailies on the same day in 1985, immediately after two nights of rioting in Handsworth in Birmingham.

What message does the photograph and its caption give to the reader about the causes of the violence and the type of people involved?

Source: The Daily Mail, *11th September, 1985*

A youth menacingly brandishes a petrol bomb

Editorials or 'comments'

Usually newspapers include a small section where the newspaper editor makes his or her own comments on the news of the day. Editorials are very rarely just factual. They usually include the editor's own interpretations and opinions. Often different newspapers have very different views on what has happened as shown by the brief passages taken from two newspapers on the day after the Handsworth riots.

Reportedly, however, community policing ceased to be quite the flavour of the year in Handsworth some time back. Having arrived earlier it departed, in some disillusion, earlier — along with at least one senior policeman, Mr David Webb, who had done much to develop the concept. Couple that reversal with a determination to have a bash at the pushers — as ordered from on high — and you may have a recipe for trouble. It is (genuinely it is) hard to draw the line between a resolute refusal to allow "merchants of powdered death" — black or white — to ply their trade unhindered and the systematic harassment of youths who hang around the local pub smoking the odd joint. After all, if drug dealing is the menace it has been portrayed as being this year, then it would be intolerable to ignore it in ghetto areas. On the other hand, to legitimise heavy policing of the ghetto areas on the ground that drugs are involved, is to invite violent unrest. There is a fine and desperately difficult line here.

What we need to know, and need to know fast, is the immediate context of Handsworth: had policing deteriorated in recent weeks? Had the drug busters banged too many heads? Is there particular, local tension between blacks and Asians and, if so, why?

Source: The Guardian, 11 Sept., '85

Could the police have gone in harder and sooner to smother the riot? Were they inhibited by the post-Scarman emphasis on softly does it?

Handsworth is acknowledged to be a centre for drug trafficking in cocaine and heroin. Why is this? Is it because police there in recent years have turned a blind eye to ganja smoking (an illegal tradition among West Indians) and so encouraged the pushers of more lethal drugs to do their evil trade in the district, too?

We have every sympathy for the police. They have a thankless and dangerous duty in trying neither to harass black youngsters unwarrantably nor to leave them to stew in their own no-go ghettoes. Have the police in Handsworth been too permissive? Is this riot, in part at least, the grisly result of an excess of good intent by the authorities over realism?

Source: Daily Mail, 11 Sept., '85

Notice that whereas *The Guardian* suggests that policing and police treatment might have been too tough and could be partly responsible for the trouble, *The Daily Mail* suggests that the police might have not been tough enough.

Language

Very often the words used in a newspaper report tell you what to think. For example, words like 'yob' and 'thug' give a very negative image of young people.

Content analysis

Where an article appears in a paper, and how much space is given to it, tells us how important it is thought to be. The Handsworth riots reports not only took up most of the front page of most papers but also filled many inside pages. Counting the space given to a particular story in a newspaper, usually measured in column inches, is known as **CONTENT ANALYSIS**. You can also use this method to see how much space a newspaper gives to different types of coverage such as news, sport, features and adverts. You may be surprised at how little 'news' there is in many papers.

Content analysis can also be used to see how newspapers treat particular groups of people such as young people or the unemployed. For example, *Today* newspaper, on Monday, 29 September, 1986, included only four articles on women. These were an article called 'Saucy sisters frozen in time' which included two photographs, two articles on Joan Collins – 'The bitch who is only a bore' and 'It's goodbye Alexis' (including a photograph) and a full page feature on women's underwear. In addition there was a photograph of Glynis Kinnock with her husband as part of an article on defence and two letters which referred to women. All of this coverage would together fill just over two pages of the thirty five page newspaper. What does this suggest to the reader about the role of women in society?

ACTIVITY

Daily Mail
WEDNESDAY, SEPTEMBER 11, 1985
20p

BLAZE RIOT SPECIAL

DAILY EXPRESS
Wednesday September 11 1985 ● 20p ● TV Pages 20 and 21 ● THE VOICE OF BRITAIN

England, 1985

Handsworth ablaze again after night of horror

D·A·L·E
GENERATING SETS

● Two die in night of arson and looting
● Angry mob force Home Secretary to dive for cover
● Hurd warns: This could hit other cities

BLOODLUST

THE GUARDIAN

Printed in London and Manchester   Wednesday September 11 1985   25p

centaur

THE Mirror

Saturday, September 11, 1985 FORWARD WITH BRITAIN   18p

Two killed and others feared dead as more violence breaks out in Handsworth

Besieged Hurd pledges riot crackdown

Police van rescues Home Secretary from fury of crowd

THE Sun
Wednesday, September 11, 1985   18p   TODAY'S TV: PAGE 12

BLITZ ISSUE
Pages 2, 3, 4, 5, 6, 14 & 15

FRONTLINE BRITAIN

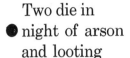

WAR ON THE STREETS

THIS was the terrifying face of Front Line Britain yesterday.

A black youth strides down the riot-torn streets of Handsworth, in Birmingham, a lighted petrol bomb in his hand.

In a nearby street, a policeman shelters behind his shield as a car blazes. It was the second day of a war in the streets of Britain's Second City which has left two dead, two others missing, and at least 45 shops petrol-bombed and looted.

A mob of 40 youths attacked cars early today in Toxteth, Liverpool—scene of some of Britain's worst riots in 1981.

● See Pages 2, 3, 14 and 15.

HATE OF A BLACK BOMBER

The above headlines appeared on the front pages of national newspapers on Wednesday, 11 September, 1985 after the Handsworth riots.

● How much information does each headline give the reader about what actually happened?
● What image of the riots does each headline create? How does the use of war imagery ('Blitz', 'Frontline Britain', etc.) influence the way you picture these events?
● Do the headlines suggest any reasons why the riots happened?
● *The Sun, The Daily Mail, The Mirror* and *The Daily Express* also carried the photo reproduced on page 65 on the front page. Taken with the headlines, what message is this giving to the reader about the riots?
● What actually happened on the two days of rioting was summarised by *The Guardian* (reproduced on the next page). Do you feel that the above headlines are a true interpretation of what happened?

How the trouble started and flared

By Martin Wainwright

6 PM MONDAY: a fight began outside the Villa Cross pub when police officers approached an Asian man about suspected motoring offences. West Indian youths came to the man's aid – after he appealed to them, according to one version; after they were outraged by police treatment of him, according to another. The man drove off in the melee.

8 30 PM: firemen were called to the Villa Cross Hall, opposite the pub. On arrival, they were warned by youths that there would be trouble if they tried to put out the fire.

8 40 PM: bricks, bottles and petrol bombs were hurled at the firemen, forcing them to withdraw. Police arrived and chased youths through back alleys as stone-throwing incidents spread.

9 PM: fires were started in lower Lozells Road, initially at a textile shop which burned fiercely.

9 30 PM: gas cylinders exploded when a garage next to the textile shop caught fire. Flames spread to neighbouring buildings. Lootings began in the absence of any major police presence and continued in Lozells Road for two hours. Several thousand rioters controlled the area and sealed it off with barricades of burning cars.

11 30 PM: fifty shops in Lozells Road and surrounding streets were on fire as police approached the hub of the riot, fighting their way through a succession of barricades. Electricity supplies to the riot area failed when water from firemen's hoses short-circuited cables.

MIDNIGHT: with few shops in the riot area not burned or looted, the rioters began to run out of steam. Firemen edged closer to the worst-affected area, deluging it with water and foam. Police were in control of most of the area but unable to prevent occasional stone-throwing and petrol bomb attacks.

3 AM TUESDAY: looters who had dropped their booty in local gardens while fleeing from police, returned discreetly to collect it. Food, clothes and other spoils were fished out of bin-liners and showed off to bystanders.

4 AM: the area returned to relative good order for the first time since rioting began.

7 AM: two bodies discovered by firemen in the half-ruined Post Office at Lozells Road. Astonished residents wandered round the area attempting to assess what happened and why.

1.30 PM: after a quiet morning with much police and political reaction on radio and TV, trouble flared again when the Home Secretary, Mr Douglas Hurd, arrived in a police convoy. Initial shouts of abuse when he attempted to talk to local people were followed by volleys of stones.

2.05 PM: the Home Secretary leaves Handsworth hurriedly in a police van after his safety becomes difficult to guarantee.

2.10 PM: burning, stone-throwing and looting spread through streets around Lozells Road. Vehicles, including a police van and an ITN car, were overturned and set on fire.

2.15 PM: stones thrown at a police car in Perry Bar, the first trouble outside Handsworth.

3 PM-7 PM: sporadic rioting continues in Handsworth with a heavy police presence preventing concentrations on the scale of the previous night. The search continues for two people unaccounted for at Lozells Road post office where the bodies were found earlier in the day.

Source: The Guardian, *11 Sept., '85*

ACTIVITY

On the evening of Tuesday, 15 April, 1986 President Reagan ordered a bombing attack on Libya in response to Libya's past terrorist activities. British air-bases were used in the attack. On the following morning the attack was the main story in all the national newspapers although the way in which they reported the event differed. The two front pages reproduced on the following pages illustrate some of the differences. Whilst one focuses on the glory of the act the other looks at it in terms of human suffering. Similarly the editorials from the same papers have different emphases.

Using the headlines, photographs, editorials and language used in the articles explain what these articles have in common and how they are different in the way they see President Reagan's act.

REAGAN'S REVENGE

MIRROR COMMENT

Enough!

WHAT was the alternative? In what other way was Colonel Gaddafi to be forced to understand that he had a price to pay for his terrorism?

The United Nations could not, and would not act.

Gaddafi's Arab neighbours, hate him though they do, were terrified of the Libyan leader's sinister influence.

European nations were willing to turn a blind eye to his terrorism because they needed his oil.

Each of them, in their spineless way, made yesterday's air attack on Libya inevitable.

Blows

They knew—but preferred not to believe—that a US President could not allow his citizens to be murdered and maimed without retaliation.

Having said that, two devastating blows have now been struck by American bombers. It is enough.

A superpower cannot go to war with a loudmouth. The remedy would be out of proportion to the grievance.

Mr Reagan is a hero at home. But one photo of an innocent child maimed by a stray bomb could lose the propaganda war for him.

Action

He and Mrs Thatcher say there is solid, irrefutable evidence that Gaddafi was planning more terrorist outrages.

They had better publish it, and quick.

Those European allies of the US wringing their hands over the bombing should now accept their own responsibility and take the diplomatic, political and economic action against Libya which they have so far shirked.

Had they acted earlier, the bombing might have been avoided.

DAILY Mirror

FORWARD WITH BRITAIN 18p

3 am: Guinness kidnap shootout

'WE DID WHAT WE HAD TO DO'

RONALD REAGAN The President of the United States addressing the American nation yesterday

REAGAN'S REVENGE

Right, Ron!

Right, Maggie!

WHAT can be done about terrorists?

Ronald Reagan shows what can be done.

Have the guts to fight back. Blast them. Allow them no hiding place even inside their own country.

The Sun applauds the courage and strength of the U.S. President.

A cost always has to be paid for standing up to evil men.

Mr Reagan has been prepared to pay that price.

We are proud, too, that after some caution, Margaret Thatcher has done the right thing.

THE SUN SAYS

By allowing American bombers to fly from their bases in Britain, she made possible the police action.

She took her decision after the Europeans, at the meeting of Foreign Ministers in The Hague, had demonstrated once more that they are a busted flush.

Here was Mad Dog Gaddafi waging a war of treachery and destruction and terror against the entire Western world.

Yet the quaking messieurs, herrenvolk and the rest could not even agree to sacrifice their precious trade with Libya.

Our own lily-white faint hearts are complaining that we have placed ourselves in the front line for retaliation.

Persecution

Have they forgotten the murdered police girl, Yvonne Fletcher? Or the killer bands Gaddafi sent to London?

Or the arrest and persecution of British citizens in Tripoli?

The truth is that we were already in the front line.

As for the Europeans, what do we have in common with President Mitterrand, who had not the backbone to allow the bombers to fly over France?

We are close to Europe only by geography.

The Atlantic is broad, but all our ties, all our ideals, all our interests bind us to the U.S.

We **CAN** destroy Gaddafi and all terrorists. We **CAN** make the world a safer and better place.

By acting together as partners and friends.

Mission accomplished ... smiling Americans at Lakenheath, Suffolk, yesterday after the raid

ACTIVITY

For at least two different newspapers on the same day select a major item of news. Then count up the amount of coverage given to this item in each newspaper and look at the headlines, photographs, editorials and words used to describe the event.

1 What image is put over by each paper?
2 Do both papers report the events in the same way or are there differences?
3 Do you think that either of your papers is biased (one-sided); why do you feel this?

Choose one of the following issues or topics:

- unemployment
- drugs
- women
- politics
- education
- crime
- teenagers

Collect copies of the same newspaper for a few days.

1 Cut out all of the articles on your subject; how much space is given it?
2 Using headlines, photographs and words used, what impression is given by the newspaper of the issue you have chosen? Do you think that this is a fair picture?

3 USING NEWSPAPERS WITH OTHER RESEARCH METHODS

So far we've looked at two ways you may use newspapers as a small part of your project to illustrate an issue or as the main part of your project where you analyse the way newspapers treat an issue or a group of people. In many projects it may be that newspapers are an important source of information but need to be used with other methods of research as well.

EXAMPLE: FOOTBALL HOOLIGANISM
Research question

- How accurate is the press coverage of football hooliganism?

Methods of research

- Content analysis of newspaper coverage
- Observation at football matches
- Questionnaire survey of supporters
- Interview with the police

EXAMPLE: POLITICAL BIAS IN NEWSPAPERS
Research questions

- Are newspapers politically biased?
- Do people choose a newspaper for its politial bias?
- Does political bias influence readers in any way?

Methods of research

- Comparison of newspapers
- Questionnaire survey of readers
- Letters to the editors of different newspapers

CHECKLIST

- If you use indexes or libraries to find newspaper articles describe exactly what you did; this is part of your research.

- Always write the date and source of any newspaper cuttings you use.

- Never use newspaper cuttings just for illustration. You should always write about these and make it clear how they fit into your enquiry.

- Try to say how accurate newspaper reports are. If possible take cuttings from different newspapers so that you can check for biased reporting.

Chapter Ten
Putting your Project Together

A Final Checklist

- Include a contents page at the front of your project listing the separate chapters.

- Write an introduction explaining why you chose the topic, what exactly you wanted to find out (your main questions or hypothesis) and how you actually did your research. (Although the introduction is included at the beginning of the project it is often best to write it quite late on when you are clear how your project is going.)

- Make sure that it is clear exactly what research you have done, even if the results of the research were not very useful. (For example you should include letters which you have written even if you received no reply.)

- Plan your chapters carefully; make sure that they follow on from each other and that there is some structure to your project. Usually chapters discussing background research come before those based on primary research such as interviews.

- Take care over presentation. Your work should be neat and well set out; it should look good. Include photographs, maps, diagrams, graphs and tapes wherever possible but do not include these things if they are not relevant.

- If you copy anything directly, or if you include photographs or tables from a book or leaflet, say underneath where you got it from (the 'source') as in this book.

- If you have kept a log book or diary with your project include it. If your log book is itself your main report, write an introduction and conclusion to go with it. Try to make your log book as attractive and varied as possible. For example, if you are keeping a log based on observation in a primary school include examples of pupils' work.

- At the end of your project write a clear and detailed conclusion. This should answer the questions which you asked in your introduction. In your conclusion you should also comment on your own research. Which parts worked well? Did you have any particular problems? How could you improve it if you had more time?

- Finally, include a bibliography. This is a list of all books, leaflets, television programmes etc. which you have used.

Appendix: Methods of Sociological Research

There are several different methods used by sociologists. This chapter looks at some of the main methods of research and at some of the strengths and weaknesses of each approach.

1 SOCIAL SURVEYS

When sociologists want to make general statements about the groups they are studying, or wish to produce facts and statistics they will use a social survey. In a social survey a large number of people are asked the same questions. Their answers are then used to draw up tables and charts like the one below taken from Peter Townsend's research on poverty.

The poor have nastier jobs		
Percentage in 1968/9 who . . .	Unskilled manual	Professional/managerial
. . . had more than two weeks paid holiday a year	9%	59%
. . . had free or subsidized meals	19%	52%
. . . had occupational pensions	24%	96%
. . . had been unemployed more than two weeks in previous 12 months	16%	0
. . . worked in 'poor' or 'very poor' conditions	40%	6%
. . . worked before 8am or at night	55%	17%
. . . had no pay when sick	63%	4%
. . . worked out of doors	63%	7%
. . . were subject to one week's notice or less	77%	4%

In this research, carried out in 1968, Townsend surveyed 2052 households to find out how much poverty there was in Britain and what sorts of people were likely to be poor. From his results he found that, in 1968, over 3 million people were living on incomes below what they could get on supplementary benefits and that a further 11.8 million were only 40% above this level.

He was also able to show that those most likely to be poor included groups such as one-parent families, the elderly and large families.

The population Census is a social survey which is filled in by every household in Britain every ten years. From this we get information on the number of people of different ages living in Britain, the size of families, type of housing etc. Most surveys, though, do not ask everyone to fill them in; this would take too long and would cost too much money. Most surveys, like Townsend's, are sample surveys. In a sample survey only part of the population being studied are asked questions. However, sociologists still want to make general statements about the group as a whole, they therefore select their sample to be representative of everyone who could be included in the research. That is, if they are only studying 10% of the population they make sure that everyone has an equal chance of being included — that there is no bias in their sample. In practice this is achieved by taking a random sample. Everyone who could be included in the survey is listed in a sampling 'frame' and names are selected from this list randomly, either by using a computer or random number tables or simply by taking, say, every tenth name on the list.

Sometimes different types of sample are used, either to make the sample more accurate or to make the research easier to carry out. A stratified sample is used when you want to be absolutely sure that certain types of people are included in the same proportion as in the population as a whole. Townsend in his research wanted to include all income levels. He therefore divided his sampling frame into high income areas, middle income areas and low income areas and sampled from each area separately. Market researchers who want to produce information very quickly often use quote samples. In these the type of people to be included in the sample to make it representative is worked out beforehand and the interviewer has to ask people who fit his or her quota. So an interviewer may be told to interview the following 'quota':

- 20 working class males aged 18—35
- 20 working class males aged 36 plus
- 20 working class females aged 18—35
- 20 working class females aged 36 plus
- 20 middle class males aged 18—35 . . .
  . . . etc.

If a sample is selected by random methods the characterics of the sample (age, sex, social class etc.) will be the same as for the population as a whole.

Many researchers carry out a check to see if their sample has introduced bias which means that their results are inaccurate. They can do this by comparing the sample to the population as a whole as shown, for example, in the Census. The table on the next page compares information and figures from three published sources.

Comparison of information from three different sources

Age	UK total population 1969 (Registrar General)	Poverty survey 1968–9	Family expenditure survey 1969	Percentage of each each group who were females		
				UK total population 1969 (Registrar General)	Poverty survey 1968–9	Family expenditure survey 1969
0–4	8·6	8·9	9·7	48	46	47
5–9	8·4	8·7	9·2	49	50	50
10–14	7·3	7·7	7·9	49	49	48
15–19	7·0	7·2	6·8	49	48	49
20–29	14·1	13·4	12·8	50	51	53
30–39	12·0	12·4	12·6	49	49	50
40–49	13·0	12·4	13·3	50	51	49
50–59	11·9	11·7	11·0	52	52	52
60–69	10·4	10·3	10·2	55	55	53
70–79	5·6	5·5	5·0	63	65	58
80+	1·8	1·8	1·4	71	70	69
Total	100	100	100	51	51	51
Number	54,395,000	6,045	20,744	—	—	—

Source: Peter Townsend, Poverty in the United Kingdom, p.955

The table above compares Townsend's sample with the actual figures for Britain's population for age and sex. As you can see his sample is very close to the actual population figures.

A social survey may be carried out using a questionnaire. Alternatively interviews can be used.

In both cases most questions are PRE-CODED; that is people answering the questions are given a list of alternative answers from which to choose. Each answer is represented by a number which can be fed into a computer for easy analysis. When large numbers of people are being surveyed ease of analysis is important. Peter Townsend's research on poverty used a questionnaire which was 39 pages long. It asked questions on all areas of family life including employment, income, style of living, health and disability. This questionnaire was filled in by trained interviewers, each interview lasting on average just over two hours. One page from this interview schedule is shown opposite.

A formal interview was also used in this way by Goldthorpe and Lockwood's research in Luton looking at the class position of affluent workers. In both these cases a formal interview was preferable to a questionnaire which people filled in themselves because the questionnaire was long and complicated and the interviewer could be present to explain any questions which were not understood. However interviews are expensive and take longer than questionnaires; of course questionnaires are more practical when the people being studied are scattered all over the country.

Writing questions which people understand and which find out exactly what the sociologist wants to know is very difficult. Therefore, for questionnaires and formal interviews, sociologists usually carry out a pilot survey before their actual survey. This involves trying out the questions on a small sample of people. If the questions are misunderstood or produce vague answers it is then possible to rewrite them before the research is carried out.

FOR ALL   CODE ALL

7. Now could I ask a few questions about food? Do you have a
    cooked breakfast most days? I mean four or   yes
    more days a week — things like bacon and egg   no
    (not porridge or toast)?   DK
                                                              Does Not Apply

(b) During the last two weeks was there a day   yes
     when you ate no cooked meal at all (I mean   no
     from getting up to going to bed)?   DK
                                                              Does Not Apply

(c) Do you have fresh meat most days, I mean
     four or more days a week (not sausages,   yes
     bacon or boiled ham) — either here or in your   no
     meals out?   CHECK ANSWER ESPECIALLY   DK
                         CAREFULLY FOR HOUSEWIFE   Does Not Apply

ASK HOUSEWIFE ONLY   CODE HOUSEHOLD ONLY

8. (a) Do you normally have a Sunday joint   yes
         i.e. three weeks out of 4)?   no
                                                              DK

(b) How many pints do you usually take for the family   no. of pints
     (everyone in the household) in a whole week,   in week
     including any extra at weekends and fresh milk bought
     from a shop?   OFFICE
                                                          USE ONLY

(c) And do you buy tinned or powdered milk as well?   yes
                                                             no
                                                             DK

ASK HOUSEWIFE ONLY   CODE HOUSEHOLD ONLY

9. (a) Do you ever buy second-hand clothing   CODE   often
         from a shop or a stall, for yourself or   ONE   sometimes
     others in the household?   ONLY   never
                                                            DK

(b) Do you buy any of your clothing or shoes
     through clubs or clothing cheques?   yes   ASK Q.9(c)
                                               no }
                                               DK }   SKIP TO Q.10

(c) About how much do you spend on clothing   WRITE IN AMOUNT IN
     clubs per week?   SHILLINGS

(d) Do you ever miss payments or pay less than   regularly
     the full amount?   not often
                                                       no
                                                       DK

ASK HOUSEWIFE ONLY   CODE HOUSEWIFE ONLY

10. Have you had a new winter coat in   Does Not Apply SKIP TO Q.11
     the last 3 years (i.e. 3 winters)?   yes
                                                 no
                                                 DK

FOR ALL   CODE ALL HOUSEHOLD

11. Has everyone got adequate footwear for   yes
    fine weather AND if it rains?   no
                                       DK
                                       Does not apply

FOR ALL

12. Can you tell me whether you

           X – smoke?   IF YES, ASK Q.12(a)   SKIP
           Y – buy a daily newspaper?   TO
           0 – regularly do the football pools (in season)?   Q.13
           1 – regularly have a flutter on the horses or dogs?
           2 none of these
           3 DK
           4 Does Not Apply

(a) How many cigarettes/ozs of tobacco a week?

☐ _____ cigs/ozs ☐ _____ cigs/ozs   OFFICE
☐ _____ cigs/ozs ☐ _____ cigs/ozs   USE

ASK HOUSEWIFE   CODE HOUSEHOLD ONLY

13. About how much did you (and your family) spend altogether last
    Christmas – I mean extra to the usual housekeeping – on
    presents, food, entertainment, everything?

                                          Estimate in £'s

Source: Poverty in the United Kingdom, *p.1159*

For both interviews and questionnaires there is the problem of non-response. What effect on results do people who refuse to reply have? Townsend's survey had an 82% response rate; this is considered high for sociological research.

When people do not reply to questionnaires, or refuse to be interviewed, this could make the sample unrepresentative. The sociologist must therefore find out as much as possible (age, sex, social class for example) about these people so that he or she can estimate how this could affect the results. Generally interviews have a higher response rate than questionnaires.

Despite their relative advantages, interviews do introduce another problem, that of **INTERVIEWER BIAS**. Research has shown that interviewees are influenced by the appearance, manner and tone of voice of interviewers and will often give the answers which they feel are expected of them. This was illustrated very clearly by a study carried out by Stuart Rice in 1914. Two thousand destitute (down and out) men were asked how they would explain their situation. Two interviewers with very different personal views were used to ask the questions. The one interviewer who was a socialist received answers which blamed the economic situation in the country whereas the other interviewer who was a prohibitionist (someone who believes that the making and sale of alcohol should be banned) received answers which blamed their position on alcohol. Clearly the men often gave the answers that they thought the interviewer wanted to hear.

So social surveys produce large quantities of statistical information which can be used to make general statements about the population cheaply and quickly.

Critics of the social survey do not only mention practical difficulties such as non-response and interviewer bias. They also make more general criticisms about the use of direct questions for getting information about society. They argue:

- To be useful a questionnaire must ask the right questions. Sociologists ask questions which they think are important. But sociologists are frequently middle class, usually over 25, often male. When studying groups who are different from themselves such as working class people or teenagers it may be that their questions actually miss many important points and their results have more to do with the questions that they have asked than with how these people actually behave. Sociologists who make this criticism would prefer to use informal interviews or participant observation.
- Closed questions leave no room for putting in what you really believe. The respondent has to tick the box or choose the option which is nearest to the answer that he or she would like to give. Even if people explain their answers the information will not be used because it cannot be fed into the computer. Therefore, critics claim that questionnaires and formal interviews may be used for getting basic facts but they cannot measure opinions or what people mean by their answers.
- There is no way of checking that people answer honestly. Goldthorpe and Lockwood in their research into affluent workers carried out two formal interviews. The first, in the workplace, was backed up with direct observation. The second, in the home, was not supported by observation. Goldthorpe and Lockwood recognise that this presents a problem:
  'It means, for example, that our information about respondents' relationships with their kin, neighbours or friends, or about their leisure activities or participation in various clubs and societies is all based upon the account that they themselves gave to us in interview and not upon our own direct study. The possibility thus exists of bias and distortion occurring in the data as a result of the respondents' attempts, conscious or otherwise, to present themselves in a certain manner ... it is wise to distinguish between what people say they do and what they in fact do.' (page 49)

2 INFORMAL INTERVIEWS

Whereas the formal interview is used to carry out large scale social surveys aimed at collecting statistical information, informal interviews are usually used on a smaller scale to get more detailed descriptive information. For an informal interview a sociologist draws up a list of topics which he or she wishes to discuss but does not write out lists of pre-coded questions which are asked in every interview. In the informal interview the researcher will make sure that these topics are covered but the interview is more like a fairly relaxed conversation guided by the sociologist than a question and answer session. In her research on the family, Elizabeth Bott interviewed twenty couples in London. They were asked about all aspects of their relationships, both inside and outside the family. Each couple was interviewed, on average, thirteen times at home.
  'Each interview began with ten minutes to an hour of casual conversation, followed by direct discussion of topics on the interview outline for an hour or longer, followed by more casual conversation at the end. The topics were used

as a general guide by the field worker (interviewer); the order of topics and the form of questioning were left to his discretion. Usually he raised a topic and the couple carried on the discussion themselves with occasional additional questions by the field worker. The discussion frequently wandered away from the assigned topic but little attempt was made to restrict such digressions, since all behaviour of the husband and wife towards one another and towards the fieldworker was held to be significant data.' (page 21)

In her research on motherhood Ann Oakley interviewed sixty-six women who were expecting their first child. Each woman was interviewed twice before and twice after the birth of the child. The average length of each interview was over two hours. She says: 'The interviews themselves were a mixture of structured, loosely structured and unstructured "guides" to conversation.' The interview schedule for each interview listed areas to discuss but no questions as such. Some direct questions were asked, but these were often used as a way of getting the woman to talk about her experiences.

Clearly this type of interview produces information which is very different from that produced by the social survey. The information is detailed and because identical questions have not been asked of everyone statistics are difficult to produce. Also, because the interviews often last for many hours over a period of time, the number of people studied is usually quite small. Bott interviewed twenty couples and Oakley sixty-six individuals (reduced to fifty-six by the end of the research.) Because of the small sample size and the informal nature of the interviews it is impossible to generalise from this type of research.

Bott claims:

'In the present research no attempt is made to produce general factual statements about a wide population of families by studying a sample. It is impossible to say that because five of the twenty families had a joint role relationship between husband and wife (where husband and wife share their roles rather than each having separate roles in the home), twenty-five per cent of all English urban families will have joint conjugal (marital) role relationships.' (page 9)

Informal interviews therefore usually produce detailed descriptive data which gives an insight into the lives of the people studied. This may be supplemented, as in Oakley's research, with statistics on some areas but this is not generally the aim of this research. The strength of this method is the fact that it can get close to the experiences of people themselves. Oakley claims:

'When I came to confront the completed interviews I was impressed by the fact that the women said it all much better and much more clearly and directly than a sociologist could ever do. . . . *Becoming a Mother* is a book about how it feels to have a first baby in the late 1970s in a large industrial city. It is a book about parenthood through the eyes of women.' (page 5)

Informal interviews do have problems apart from the small sample and inability to generalise. The most important of these is the question of interviewer bias. This is likely to be a larger problem than for formal interviews because the interviews are longer and more relaxed, there is not a standard list of questions and it is far more difficult for the interviewer to hide his or her own opinions. Bott recognises this problem but suggests that rather than trying to avoid it the interviewer must try to understand how bias affects the data.

'It is obvious that neither the research couples nor the field workers were objective (unbiased) about the research in the sense of not being emotionally involved in it and with each other. The research relationship could not have been maintained over a period of months, and even years in some cases, without serious emotional involvement on both sides ... We were treated more or less as friends and we in turn developed friendly feelings for our informants ... our aim was not to eliminate emotional involvement but to understand it and to find out how it affected the data.' (page 41)

Oakley also addresses this problem:

'Once you start to study people it is at least a possibility that they become influenced by the fact of being studied, that their behaviour and attitudes are changed and the whole point of doing the research is lost.' (page 310)

In her own research Oakley found that many of her interviewees actually asked her questions about her own experiences of motherhood and used her to talk through their own worries. At the end of the study she asked the interviewees: 'Do you feel that being involved in this research – my coming to see you – has affected your experience of becoming a mother in any way?' Their answers are summarised below:

'No' – 27%
'Yes' – 73%

Thought about it more	30%
Found it reassuring	25%
Relief to talk	30%
Changed attitudes/behaviour	7%

Note: Total adds up to more than 100% because some people gave more than one answer.

A Mass Observation Archive interviewer during the Second World War

However Oakley defended her interviewing method. She argued that it was impossible to get detailed personal information without a relationship of trust — thus the interviewer cannot avoid becoming involved in the interview.

3 PARTICIPANT OBSERVATION

Participant observation is an attempt to gain an understanding of the group being studied by actually taking part in their everyday lives. Researchers who support this method feel that you can only fully understand a situation by being part of it and observing for yourself what actually happens. Other methods of research are thought to be unreliable for two main reasons:

- In asking questions the sociologist must decide what he or she thinks is important. In many cases this might be wrong yet people cannot reply outside of the coded answers or answer questions which are not there. Therefore, the findings of the research are limited by the questions asked. Whyte, who observed a street corner gang in America, says: 'As I sat and listened, I learned answers to questions that I would not even have had the sense to ask if I had been getting my information solely on an interviewing basis.' (page 303)
- Answers to questions are unreliable partly because people may give the answer that they want to believe about themselves rather than the truth and partly because people are sometimes unaware of their own behaviour. For example, observation has shown that many teachers spend more time with male students than with female students although this is something of which they are unaware.

The strength of participant observation as a method of research lies in its ability to overcome these problems and to provide detailed information which describes how people actually behave. Very often this information could not have been gained by any other method of research.

There are, however, clear difficulties facing a participant observer. First the observer must become accepted by the group that he or she wants to observe. In *Street Corner Society* Whyte was introduced to a contact — Doc — who gave him entry to the group; so long as he was with Doc no one asked any questions. In his research on football hooliganism in Leicester John Williams spent a long period of time involving himself in the local community playground and the local probation centre to make contacts. In both these situations the researchers were open about their research. This is known as overt participant observation. In some cases sociologists have disguised their role as an observer and have pretended to be an ordinary participant. This is known as covert participant observation and raises the moral or ethical problem of whether it is fair to 'spy' on people in this way. This method was used by James Patrick in *Glasgow gang observed* and is generally used when permission to study the group openly would possibly not be given. An example might be a religious sect. Having got into the group the observer needs to fit in. This involves learning the norms of the group. One common problem here is the need not to constantly ask questions.

A second problem is that the observer must decide how involved in the group he or she should become. Ideally the observer should become involved enough to be accepted, but should keep enough distance to be able to observe properly. During a long period of observation it is possible that the observer could become so involved with the group that he or she starts taking things for granted and therefore becomes a poor observer. Whyte says:

'I began as a non-participating observer. As I became accepted into the community, I found myself becoming almost a non-observing participant. I got the feel of life in Cornerville, but that meant that I got to take for granted the same things that my Cornerville friends took for granted.' (page 321)

How involved to become presents a problem on another level, when becoming involved could actually change people's behaviour. John Williams found this problem when he was asked to become captain of the local football team; this role involved, among other things, selecting the team. In the end Williams felt that this did not affect his role as an observer but, as a rule, participant observers are advised not to take an active role in the community they are studying. Involvement may present problems in studies of gangs or groups who are involved in law-breaking activities. The sociologist must avoid becoming involved in such activities but must do so in such a way that he or she does not raise the suspicions of other people in the group, especially if the observation is covert.

A third major problem is that the research itself may change the situation being studied. This could happen, as found by Hargreaves in his research in a secondary modern school, because people act differently when they know they are being watched. During his research Hargreaves observed in a number of classrooms. He says:

'A few of the teachers acted with some kind of withdrawal ... whenever I went into a lesson conducted by Mr H, he made the boys work quietly out of text books, talked in a whisper to boys at his desk so that I could not hear from the back and declined to speak to the class as a whole unless this became unavoidable ... Many of the teachers appeared to behave quite naturally and act as if I was not in the room at all, and it is difficult to check on the extent of changes my presence produced. Sometimes the teachers would themselves indicate the effect of my presence. In the lower streams in particular the boys are caned comparatively frequently, if the conversations over lunch and in the common room are any measure of this. But it was noticeable how very rarely a teacher caned a boy while I was in the room. One day, as I was leaving the room, Mr G. said to me 'They've got a bit noisy haven't they? I think I'll cane a few when you've gone.' A further check came from conversations with the boys, who revealed changes which might otherwise have been not at all obvious ... "They put on a show for you." "They put the good act on." "Smiles and all that, and when you're gone out ...".' (pages 196–7)

In Whyte's research he involved Doc so much in his research that he influenced the way in which Doc himself behaved:

'Doc found the experience of working with me interesting and enjoyable and yet the relationship had its drawbacks. He once commented: "You've slowed me up plenty since you've been down here. Now when I do something I have to think what Bill Whyte would want to know about it and how I can explain it. Before I used to do things by instinct".' (page 301)

The observer can also influence the situation by taking part in the activities him/herself as when Williams became captain of the football team. This is illustrated in Eileen Barker's study of the Unification Church as discussed in *The making of a Moonie*. During her research Barker participated in a number of workshops organised by the Moonies as well as living in various centres with the members. She accepts that her presence did often influence the situation. The passage below describes one extreme example of this:

'I was on a twenty-one day course at which the participants were expected to deliver a lecture. The subject I was allocated was "the purpose of the coming of the messiah". I did not exactly enjoy this aspect of my research, but, participant observation does involve participation, so I gave the talk ... When I had finished a member of the audience declared that she had been extremely worried about that particular part of the doctrine, but she now understood it, and she fully accepted that the Reverend Moon (the founder of the Unification Church) was indeed the messiah. I was horrified. "But I don't believe it," I insisted. "I don't think it's true". "Perhaps not," interrupted the Moonie in charge, "but God has used Eileen to show Rosemary the truth".' (page 24)

How to record observations is a problem which the participant observer must face throughout his or her research. It is usually impossible to take notes or to use a tape recorder so the researcher must rely on memory. This could introduce the problems of bias since the observer is unlikely to remember everything.

Moonies, observed by Eileen Barker in her research

The participant observers study one group of people at a particular point in time. Also what they observe and what they see as important will depend upon the sociologist's own values. It would be impossible to repeat a study with a different observer and produce identical results. All of this means that the findings of participant observation research cannot be used to make general statements about the population as a whole. Participant observation studies provide detailed and often fascinating accounts of the lives of a particular group of people. These accounts contain information which could not possibly be got from any other method; they get as near as is possible to people's actual experiences, but the results from one gang study, for example, cannot be used to make statements about all gangs.

4 ANALYSIS OF SECONDARY DATA

The three methods discussed so far are all examples of primary research where the sociologist collects his or her own information first hand. Many sociologists, however, rather than doing primary research analyse information which already exists; this is secondary data. The sources of information which a sociologist can use include statistics produced by the government and other organisations. This may be crime statistics, divorce statistics or details of births, marriages and deaths; also used are diaries or autobiographies, newspapers, historical records and research which has been carried out by other sociologists in the past. An example of the use of secondary data is the work of Peter Laslett to test the widely believed idea that, before the industrial revolution, families were extended (including relatives such as aunts and uncles and grandparents) and that families became nuclear (including parents and children only) after industrialisation.

Laslett studied historical records on family size in England from 1564 to 1821 and showed that only about ten per cent of families could be regarded as extended. The main reasons for using secondary data for this research were that the information was readily available and was cheap to analyse. Sometimes secondary data is the only way of getting information on a topic, as, for example, with historical documents.

Whatever sources of information are used for secondary analysis there are two problems facing the sociologist. First the data has been collected for other reasons and may not include all of the information that the sociologist needs to test his or her hypothesis. Second the information may itself contain biases and inaccuracies. Diaries and letters, for example, are very personal documents and only include what the author chooses to put in. Accounts in newspapers usually concentrate on sensational events rather than day-to-day happenings and are also likely to reflect the political bias of the paper. Historical records are not always complete.

These problems can best be shown by looking at Emile Durkheim's classic study of suicide carried out at the end of the last century. Durkheim analysed the official statistics on suicide for different countries in Europe between the years 1866 and 1878. He wanted to find out what sorts of people were likely to commit suicide. To test part of his hypothesis he needed to know the religion of suicide victims; unfortunately this was not recorded in the official statistics. Durkheim therefore had to compare areas which were mostly Protestant with those which were mostly Catholic to test his hypothesis that Catholics were less likely to commit suicide than Protestants because they were more strongly involved in their church. Obviously if he had collected his information himself he would have recorded religion.

A far greater problem is the possible bias within the statistics themselves. Douglas and Atkinson have separately discussed research which shows that suicide statistics are not totally accurate. A coroner, when faced with a death, has to decide whether it is a suicide or not. If he has any doubts he will record a verdict of accidental death. Coroners do not always make the same decisions. One state in America was found to have a particularly low suicide rate. On investigation it was found that the coroner only returned a verdict of 'suicide' if a note had been left. Other research has shown that only about one-third of suicide victims leave a note. It has also been suggested that the lower suicide rate for Catholics may be because Catholic families are more likely to disguise a suicide and get a verdict of accidental death because suicide is against their religion. The fact that the statistics are not totally accurate must, in turn, raise questions about Durkheim's own research since it was based entirely on statistics.

The extent to which the problem of bias exists depends to some extent on the data being used. It is unlikely that census data and details of births, marriages and deaths in Britain today are biased. However, the same figures for Britain in the past, or for some other countries, may be unreliable. Data produced by the Census in Britain is in fact quite widely used to compare different groups of people and to show changes in society over time. Because every household is included it is ideal for this type of research.

Because of the problems with secondary data, many sociologists have chosen to use statistics and documents as a topic for study rather than as a way of testing their own hypotheses. So sociologists have, for example, studied crime statistics to find ways in which these are biased and why. This approach has been used for a lot of research into the mass media (newspapers, television, radio etc.) Rather than using information from newspapers and television to test their hypotheses, sociologists have studied the media themselves to see whether they produce a fair or biased picture of social life. This type of research usually uses the method of content analysis. This involves counting up the number of times different issues or words or people appear in the media. One example of this sort of research is that carried out by the Glasgow Media Group on television coverage of industrial relations. They recorded all television news programmes over a period of time to show how industrial conflict was shown. They found that the picture reported by the news was misleading.

References

Eileen Barker, *The making of a Moonie – choice or brainwashing?*, Basil Blackwell, 1984.

Elizabeth Bott, *Family and Social Network*, The Tavistock Press, 1957.

Emile Durkheim, *Suicide* (ed. G. Simpson), Routledge and Kegan Paul, first published in 1897.

Glasgow University Media Group, *Bad News*, Routledge and Kegan Paul, 1976.

Goldthorpe, J.H., Lockwood, D., Bechhofer, E. and Platt, J. (1969), *The Afffluent Worker in the Class Structure*, Cambridge University Press, 1969.

David Hargreaves, *Social relations in a secondary school*, Routledge and Kegan Paul, 1967.

Ann Oakley, *From here to maternity – becoming a mother*, Martin Robertson, 1979, and *Women confined – towards a sociology of childbirth*, Martin Robertson, 1980.

Stuart Rice – discussed in 'On errors in surveys' by W.E. Deming in *Research Methods* (ed. B.J. Franklin and H.W. Osborne-Wadsworth), Belmont, 1971.

Peter Townsend, *Poverty in the United Kingdon*, Allen Lane, 1979.

W.F. Whyte, *Street Corner Society* (3rd edn.), University of Chicago Press, 1981.

John Williams, 'Notes on Research Methods', working paper, Leicester University, 1982.

Key Terms

Acknowledgements

For permission to reproduce copyright material the author and publisher are indebted to: Basil Blackwell Ltd for an extract from *The Making of a Moonie* by Eileen Barker and the Unification Church for the relevant photographic material; *The Guardian* for an article by Martin Wainwright entitled 'How the Trouble Started and Flared' and 'Handsworth, Policing and Police Treatment' both dated 11 Sept., 1985; The Controller of HMSO for 'Birth Statistics in 1984' and 'Adult Cigarette Smoking' from *Social Trends* and a sample copy of a census form; Library Association Publishing for a list of reports on Drug Abuse listed in the British Humanities Index, March 1986; Mirror Group Newspapers for 'We did what we had to do', 'Enough' from *Mirror Comment*, dated 16 April, 1986 and articles and captions from *The Scourge, a Heroin Special*, dated November 1984 and from the Handsworth riots, dated 11 Sept., 1985; the National Anti-Vivisection Society for an extract from 'Opren's Demise, Bulletin 19 — Lord Dowding Fund'; New Society Ltd for a table and questionnaire from *New Society* Magazine, 1986; Penguin Books Ltd for 'Table A2. 1 and Appendix 10; 'Questionnaire on Household Resources and Standards of Living in the UK 1968–1969' from *Poverty in the United Kingdom* by Peter Townsend (Allen Lane/Pelican Books 1979 © P. Townsend); *Radio Times* for a Grandstand cutting, 31 Jan., 1987; Research Defence Society for an article entitled 'Diabetes: Research Triumphs'; *The Sun* for cuttings entitled 'Thrilled to Blitz' and 'Right, Ron! Right Maggie!' from 'The Sun Says', both dated 16 April, 1986; Tavistock Publications for two extracts from *Family and Social Network* by Elizabeth Bott; The Times Newspapers for 'Hurd Pelted on Tour of Riot Devastation', dated 11 Sept., 1985 and an article entitled 'The Hidden Crime Wave' by Martin Kettle dated 13 Feb., 1983 and an entry from *The Times Index*; The publishers of the 1982 edition of Whitaker's Almanack for an extract from 'Addresses and details on Government and Public Offices.'

The following photo sources are acknowledged:
p.7 Nigel Luckhurst; *p.8 (top right)* Syndication International; *p.16 (top)* Nigel Luckhurst, *(bottom)* Format; *p.24* Nigel Luckhurst; *p.25 (left)* Nigel Luckhurst, *(top right)* Popperfoto, *(bottom right)* BBC Hulton; *p.32* Format; *p.33* The Unification Church; *p.36* Format; *p.45* Format; *p.51 (left)* BBC Hulton, *(right)* Format; *p.55* Nigel Luckhurst; *p.61* Sally & Richard Greenhill; *p.65* The Press Association, *p. 81* BBC Hulton, *p.84* The Unification Church.

Charts and diagrams by Chartwell Illustrators.

Cartoons and line drawings by Jane Cope.